Towards a universal basic income for all humanity

Mohammed Sofiane Mesbahi

ALSO BY THE AUTHOR

Heralding Article 25: A people's strategy for world transformation

The intersection of politics and spirituality in addressing the climate crisis

Copyright © 2020 Mohammed Sofiane Mesbahi

The moral right of the author has been asserted.

Apart from any fair dealing for the purposes of research or private study, or criticism or review, as permitted under the Copyright, Designs and Patents Act 1988, this publication may only be reproduced, stored or transmitted, in any form or by any means, with the prior permission in writing of the publishers, or in the case of reprographic reproduction in accordance with the terms of licences issued by the Copyright Licensing Agency. Enquiries concerning reproduction outside those terms should be sent to the publishers.

Matador
9 Priory Business Park,
Wistow Road, Kibworth Beauchamp,
Leicestershire. LE8 0RX
Tel: 0116 279 2299
Email: books@troubador.co.uk
Web: www.troubador.co.uk/matador
Twitter: @matadorbooks

ISBN 978 1838594 114

British Library Cataloguing in Publication Data.
A catalogue record for this book is available from the British Library.

Printed and bound in Great Britain by 4edge Limited
Typeset in 11pt Adobe Garamond Pro by Troubador Publishing Ltd, Leicester, UK

Matador is an imprint of Troubador Publishing Ltd

First Edition

'The conception of a universal basic income can remain so simple in our hearts, if each and every member of this movement perceives that the real substance of a basic income policy is, in fact, love. It seems we are always dynamic in responding to ideas, but why are we not so dynamic when it comes to love? If we feel the resonance of this idea in our hearts, it means we have already responded, how-ever unconsciously or incipiently, to the call for love.'

—Mohammed Sofiane Mesbahi

Contents

Editor's preface	xi
Introduction: 'Everyone has the right to live'	xiii
Part I: The threat of a dystopian future	1
Part II: Missing elements for a people's strategy	13
Part III: The inner dimensions of world transformation	29
Part IV: A definitively universal vision	43
Epilogue: Some final words of encouragement	53
Endnotes	73
About the author	95

Editor's preface

The following publication is written as part of an ongoing series of studies released by Share The World's Resources (STWR) which explore critical global issues from a more holistic outlook than the usual political and economic analyses. This particular book is closely related to two recent works by Mohammed Sofiane Mesbahi that also examine popular intellectual discourses in a similar way, namely the contemporary ideas of 'the commons' and 'the sharing economy'. Yet the growing cause for a universal basic income is perhaps the most tangible demand for economic sharing in the present day, even though few advocates contemplate the definitive vision of a basic income in the truly 'universal' or planetary sense—as indeed Mesbahi sets out to do in this unique investigation of the subject.

While principally aimed at activists within the basic income movements across the world, it is also hoped that anyone interested in this subject can read and benefit from the author's far-reaching observations. With this in mind, a number of explanatory and contextual notes are included at the end to help clarify where STWR stands on some of the more technical issues, and also to help provide some introductory material for interested newcomers to this important (although somewhat controversial) policy proposal.

For those who have read any of Mesbahi's previous publications, it will be clear that identical themes are focused upon and further elaborated here, particularly around the need for continuous worldwide demonstrations that uphold *Article 25* of the Universal Declaration of Human Rights. This is, after all, our founding purpose and essential vision as a campaigning organisation. However, Mesbahi also seeks to elucidate this proposition by focusing on, in his words, the 'inner side' or 'psychological-spiritual' dimensions of world transformation. Any repetitions of the same themes and observations are therefore entirely intentional on the part of the author, given the fact that we are still far from realising a transformational vision of all people and nations coming together to share the world's resources.

If the simple reasoning of this study is contemplated with an open heart and mind, then the sympathetic reader may find that the repetition of certain themes serves to bring greater awareness about the nature of the world problem, as well as a clearer sense of the solution. A solution, as Mesbahi repeatedly asserts throughout his writings, that is 'forever embedded in the hearts of everyone.' In this light, the feasibility of the vision set out on these pages is not a matter of intellectual debate. For it is nothing more than a *call to action* that only we ourselves, both individually and collectively, can ultimately respond to and co-create.

London, UK, January 2020

INTRODUCTION

'Everyone has the right to live'

'We have tried every other strategy and nothing else will work, unless nations freely share their surplus wealth with an awareness of divinity, of the one Humanity, the one Love. That is the key we are all searching for, which has forever been embedded in the hearts of everyone.'

Of all the emerging debates on the economic policies that embody the principle of sharing, there is one proposal that stands out for its uniqueness and simplicity: the call for a universal basic income (UBI). A growing literature propounds the ethical and philosophical justifications for this enduring idea, as well as its practical applicability within both the major industrialised and less developed nations. Until now, however, the progressive notion of a basic income has yet to be implemented in its definitively universal form within any world region, notwithstanding the small-scale pilot schemes and limited national systems that are endlessly cited in contemporary debates. Hence the purpose of this enquiry is to examine the prospects for achieving an inspiring vision of 'freedom from want' for every person on Earth, all of whom should be entitled to receive a regular, individual and unconditional monetary transfer that is sufficient to ensure an adequate standard of living *in perpetuity*.[1]

Is it realistic to believe we can ever achieve this apparently utopian dream in all countries, which must also be envisioned alongside the universal provision of public services and other social benefits: free healthcare and essential medicines; free education at every level; free childcare provision for every pre-schooler; ample supplementary benefits for old-age care and people with disabilities; adequate support for everyone to afford decent housing; subsidised public utilities and good quality public transport; and more?[2] We have previously investigated the need for *Article 25* of the Universal Declaration of Human Rights to be established as a foundational law within each country, supervised by the United Nations with the all-inclusive backing of world public opinion.[3,4] In this regard, is the prospect of enshrining a basic income as an individual legal right one of the surest means for guaranteeing the comprehensive realisation of *Article 25* for every man, woman and child?[5] And can we ultimately envisage the right to a basic income being realised in the truly universal sense, whereby nations cooperate on a multilateral level to ensure that every government can provide their citizens with access to the necessities for a dignified life?

Without doubt, the implications of executing this simple social policy instrument are immense and potentially transformative, especially when we consider the possibility of permanently ending global poverty via some form of international redistributive mechanism.[6] Yet it is not the intention of our enquiry to examine in detail the technical considerations around how a basic income should be constituted within different nations, or the arguments against targeting and conditionality, or indeed the forward-thinking debates regarding options for funding through progressive taxation or more innovative measures. Suffice to say, enough literature already makes a compelling case for a new system of income distribution for the 21st century, in light of the inefficiencies and shortcomings of means-tested welfare systems throughout the world.[7] We shall assume the reader already agrees that new solutions are needed for tackling poverty and inequality, which can no longer be realistically addressed through the established social objective of full employment based on continuous economic growth. The eventual necessity of disassociating everyone's income from wage labour alone is predictable for many compelling reasons, not least the mounting pressures of technological change and an inequitable model of economic globalisation.[8]

Based on this analysis, the prominent arguments for introducing a basic income in every country—aiming towards the highest possible amount that is sufficient to guarantee an adequate standard of living—should be taken extremely seriously by informed scholars, activists and policymakers.[9] The moral case for realising such an entitlement from birth is central to the founding ideals of our organisation, Share The World's Resources (STWR): that the Earth is a shared inheritance which equally belongs to everyone, thus conferring upon society a responsibility to fairly distribute and conserve nature's produce in accordance with egalitarian principles. This rationale is notably reflected in the works of Thomas Paine, Henry George, G.D.H. Cole and many other distinguished writers, who variously conceived of the land and natural resources as part of our collective wealth, which is invariably derived from the combined labour, creativity and achievements of society as a whole and earlier generations.[10] Hence it is reasonable to argue that everyone should be entitled to share in the fruits of our common heritage (including the modern-day benefits of technological progress), which can be directly realised by instituting a policy of 'social dividends' payable to all citizens as an economic right.[11]

The underlying principle behind how to achieve this venerable aim could not be simpler: every nation needs to create a common pool of resources that can provide for the essential needs of all, which is facilitated and funded by members of the whole society (according to respective means and ability). We already see that principle in operation in many of our social and economic institutions, however fragile and partial such historical attainments may be. But we have reached a time when the principle of sharing has to be applied as the foundation of economic activity within all nations, all regions and eventually throughout the entire world community, if humanity's evolutionary progress is to be safeguarded for future generations. It is in this light that we shall investigate the implications of distributing a full basic income to all, and not just in the usual political and academic terms.

Drawing on a more holistic outlook, we can also view the longstanding efforts to institute a new social settlement as an expression of maturity, responsibility and even love within this painfully divided world. Know that to entertain the very idea of achieving the highest vision of a UBI is, in itself, an expression of intelligence and common sense that arises from one's inherent maturity, responsibility and love; for what else can such a vision reflect in these grossly unequal times, if not our unsuppressed conscience that says 'everyone has the right to live'? It appears that many participants within the basic income movement are motivated by an intuitive belief that the world can be such a freer, more creative and joyful place, as there is obviously so much wealth and material produce that is unfairly shared among a relatively small minority of the world population. So the very idea of applying the principle of sharing to our economic problems, as realised through a UBI and manifold other redistributive policies, is to give concrete substance and structure to the aspirations enshrined in the Universal Declaration of Human Rights. When viewed through such a lens, the meaning of a UBI is not merely to ensure 'the right to live', for it can also be understood in the following terms: as the art of creating balance in the world's social and economic affairs, until 'right human relationship' is an established reality in our everyday lives.

PART I

The threat of a dystopian future

Let us now examine the prospects for achieving the most comprehensive vision of a UBI worldwide, using the simple logic of our common sense and without resorting to complex intellectual arguments. On the surface, it may appear theoretically possible to implement a full UBI—at least in every highly industrialised country where established tax systems are already able to generate enough revenue to fund a universal social welfare system.[12] But we also have to ask ourselves a pertinent question: can we rely on the government of any country today to voluntarily prioritise the common needs of all their citizens? The history of social protection in the twentieth century may attest to huge improvements in the lives of millions of people, yet we now remain entrenched in a climate of financial austerity, declining public services and growing poverty in the majority of the world's nations, despite the vast amount of wealth that is continually amassed by billionaires and large corporations.

Although humanity is producing more wealth and resources than ever before in history, most developed nations remain preoccupied with selling armaments and increasing their international competitiveness through inequitable trade arrangements, rather than striving to guarantee everyone's basic socioeconomic rights through the universal provision of public goods and unconditional monetary transfers. What will therefore happen to this modest proposal for economic sharing, if there is an escalation of war or another global financial catastrophe? We can be sure that the vulgar words 'national security' will soon be invoked to defend our government's self-interested priorities, as we have already observed with the callous response of European leaders to the record influx of impoverished refugees and migrants.

Another question to ask is whether it is realistic to implement a full UBI policy today, when every society is subsumed by a dark and irrepressible influence that we have previously defined as the forces of commercialisation.[13] The term 'globalisation' is insufficient to describe the iniquitous nature of these forces that now dominate our political and economic institutions, forces that are divisive, destructive and violent to the point of being inhuman. Many advocates for a basic income certainly understand the magnitude of this problem, even though we are apt to interpret it in misleading academic terms as the outcome of mass consumerism or so-called neoliberal capitalism. It is as if we have been distracted and deluded by unbridled market forces, which is the underlying factor that has given rise to the pervasive influence of commercialisation in recent decades, poisoning our politics, our societies, our values and collective behaviours. Indeed at the root of the world problem is not only a political ideology or certain modes of economic organisation, but our self-centred attitudes and intentions that make us all susceptible to commercialisation in its myriad of forms. Thus from the most basic psychological assessment, we can observe that one of the biggest hurdles to realising a UBI in any nation today, however rich or poor, is the pursuit of profit and wealth that dominates our social structures and our everyday lives.[14]

How then shall we introduce a full basic income policy that ensures no-one lives in poverty, when everyone is somewhat conditioned by these profit-driven forces that compel us towards materialistic, competitive and atomising behaviours? There is a symptomatic element in our societies that results from this prevalent mentality, which we call indifference—an indifference that is given physical expression in the complex administration of means-tested welfare schemes, with all their associated consequences of stigmatisation and punishment by government-appointed bureaucrats. We cannot just blame a lack of 'political will' for preventing a UBI from succeeding, when we all play a part in prolonging the systemic impasse by inadvertently conforming with this status quo.

What do we think will happen if every citizen is given an obligation-free cash benefit each month, when our governments are privatising public assets and selling armaments to authoritarian regimes, and constantly manoeuvring to control the resources of weaker or dependent nations overseas? Through causing death and destruction with their covert foreign policies, many nations are in fact sustaining the idea of the 'right to kill', not the 'right to live'. And through our collective indifference and conformity, a vast proportion of the public continues to vote for these same types of politician, thus lending their energy to the established thinking and attitudes that perpetuate the whole state of affairs.

Is it therefore sufficient to give every adult a sum equivalent to say $1,000 per month, as if we can expect the wider problems of the world to subsequently resolve by themselves?

The more UBI money I demand from my government in this existing social order, the more I must expect the trends of commercialisation, global warfare and competition over resources to worsen by a corresponding measure. For the more money I may duly receive as a statutory entitlement, the more stress and imbalance will inevitably be created by my government, who continues to pursue the same ruthlessly competitive and profit-driven approach to policymaking. And the more stress I experience in this increasingly dysfunctional society, the more I shall seek financial security and demonstrate a complacent response to the world's problems.

Such is the nature of the vicious circle, even in hypothetical terms. But in reality, will any level of a basic income be high enough while these pernicious trends are concurrently worsening? For the more governments persist with their commercialising and militaristic strategies, the more expensive life will become in the ever-shrinking public sphere. Until in the end, no-one can meet their basic rights to adequate food, healthcare, housing and education with $1,000 a month or even more, regardless of how frugally they try to live. And do we really believe that any government today is likely to redistribute equitable payments of such an amount to all citizens, rather than increasing its military budget in a time of nuclear weapons proliferation, climate upheaval and resurging nationalistic attitudes?

We might see how simple it could be to implement a national-level UBI, if only the government and public could reach a consensus on what should be done. Achieving a more equal and inclusive society has always come down to very simple ideas of sharing resources through collective means, however impossible it may become in a complex society driven by the opposite principles of individualistic competition and self-interest.

Just imagine that a husband and wife are fiercely arguing in the street, and it requires an outside observer to intervene and remind them who they are. Thus the bonds of love between that couple may be restored, which by a wider analogy might apply to the relationship between politicians and the public at large, if only both expressed the same values of goodwill and mutual support. Perhaps then we would see the principle of sharing expressed throughout the entire body politic, based on the common sense understanding that there is enough food and resources for everyone, and no-one need live in penury or starve. But sadly we must account for the reality of governments who avidly thirst for power, and a disparate citizenry that largely fails to support those few politicians who stand for economic sharing as the fundamental basis of our social contract.

Hence the conditions have long been set for commercialisation to reign in world affairs, as enabled by the fight between conflicting political 'isms' and the complacency of the general populace. So complex has society become with all the laws that facilitate commercialisation and institutionalised greed, that even the most visionary politician with the right intentions is powerless to push a genuine UBI policy through any congress or parliament. Without the people of the world standing firmly behind them, the pioneers for a basic income guarantee are left begging for their idea before non-interested governments who remain ever servile to multinational corporations. And what chance do we have of persuading these governmental administrations amidst the divisions sustained by age-old vested interests, polarised ideologies and a widespread public indifference? There may be enough resources in the world for everyone to enjoy at least a minimal standard of living, but it is impossible to share that wealth more equitably within the governing paradigm of commercialisation. We might say that it is a compelling possibility that will remain a utopian impossibility, unless there is a significant change of thinking among our political leadership, coupled with a marked expansion of awareness throughout society as a whole.

This sums up our paradoxical situation, when the need for a UBI has never been greater or more important in this age of automation, with new technologies rapidly usurping millions of jobs. As long as present trends continue, then major corporations are liable to benefit from the onset of mass technological unemployment, for then they will no longer need to be concerned with paying decent wages or complying with hard-fought workers' rights. Take these as prophetic words, as we can be sure that large market-driven enterprises have no interest in the vagaries of the jobless poor, or the gradual establishment of right human relationship through implementing an economic model based on a just redistribution of co-owned wealth. From within the confines of this exploitative system, obviously we cannot count on any government to implement a basic income on our behalf, when they are more concerned with slashing benefits and employment regulations than protecting the established rights of insecure workers.

All these self-destructive tendencies are set to rapidly worsen, until the continuing growth of the world population becomes the greatest barrier to achieving a robust UBI. This is a case of straightforward economics, for what government can guarantee a liveable income stream to an amount of legal residents that may increase by many millions each year? Unquestionably, the predicted rise of the population to over 11 billion this century will forestall many visions for a balanced and sustainable world.[15] There is little hope of fairly sharing each nation's wealth among its whole population, for example, if the citizens of that nation cannot share the roads anymore due to the sheer amount of traffic congestion. Or are we willing to accept a global one-child policy as an overriding condition for implementing a UBI in every country? At the same time, are we willing to accept the continued rise of billionaires who seek to amass ever-increasing wealth, in order to sustain the ever-increasing need of government revenue to fund a maximal social state? Surely it won't be long until the world itself cannot sustain this continued assault on its resources, rendering the prospect of a UBI into a mathematical and physical impossibility, regardless of its current political infeasibility.

If we concur with the above reasoning, we have to conclude that this simple policy proposal can only plausibly succeed in a limited measure that inevitably corrupts over time. Just as the universal social services in developed countries are widely being corrupted from their originating principles and ideals, so will the introduction of a basic income be corrupted and diverted from its transformative potential—presuming it holds any chance at all within this corruptive paradigm of rampant commercialisation, militarisation and unmitigated population growth. Bearing in mind that leading multinational corporations are wealthier and more powerful than many governments, any basic income scheme that establishment politicians invent is likely to be set as low as possible, perhaps in line with the libertarian views of free market ideologues like Friedrich Hayek and Milton Friedman. If left unchecked, perhaps the trends we have outlined will reach such a peak that nations will be forced to implement a meagre basic income in response to social unrest and even violent uprisings, which may inevitably result from soaring levels of joblessness and economic insecurity alongside the flagrant luxury of the few.

Then we must also contemplate a dystopian vision of the future, where societies become like an open prison that is run on the basis of maintaining law and order among a subordinate population. Indeed, when an inmate arrives in prison to serve a long custodial sentence, they may have no happiness or hope for the future, but at least they have the certainty of being provided with the basic necessities needed to survive. Already for many people in the world, especially those who live in the most impoverished villages and shantytowns throughout the global South, there is no hope whatsoever for what tomorrow has in store. Many do not even have the same rights as prisoners, in a certain sense, if they do not have a roof over their heads or know where their next meal is coming from. Such a destitute person may agree theoretically that the world's resources should belong to everyone, but what hope do they have of receiving their fair and due entitlement, when those resources are being accumulated and controlled by a fast decreasing percentage of the planet's inhabitants?

Clearly the numbers of the marginalised and dispossessed will continue to surge under these prevailing conditions, leading to a loss of hope and further misery for a growing swathe of humanity, in the richest as well as the poorest societies. If the only response of governments is a minimum-level UBI within national borders, combined with a progressively shrunken and privatised system of social services, then the outlook for what lies ahead in the 21st century is appallingly bleak and foreboding. We may look back in 80 years' time and consider it a miracle that welfare states ever existed. For then we shall be living in a world that is exclusively dedicated to protecting the wealth of a privileged elite, who exist in a reality disconnected from the generalised privation of the subjugated majority.

PART II

Missing elements for a people's strategy

It is important to reiterate that the idea of a liveable income stream paid by the state to all citizens is a compelling and visionary proposal for our time. Yet it remains unrealistic to implement a UBI as a policy tool for creating a freer society when our governments are beholden to powerful corporate interests, the arms industry in particular. The dominance of 'profit over people' represents a formidable battle that has engaged political activists for many centuries, and it has never been more foreboding and urgent than now. Therefore our enquiry concerns how we can transform the reigning paradigm of commercialisation, so that a high-level UBI becomes a viable and incorruptible prospect—not only in the most industrialised nations, but ultimately in every country of the world.

With this in mind, our first consideration is the need for a monumental amount of public support behind the UBI cause, remembering that our primary reason for promoting a basic income is to ensure 'the right to live'. As we have argued, this radical proposition will never be upheld by our existing governments, even if some honourable politicians attempt to do so; hence it is a cause that must belong to ordinary people themselves. And the only way to bring about a fundamental change in political orthodoxy and social attitudes is through immense, non-stop demonstrations for an end to extreme human deprivation, which is where the road to achieving an emancipatory form of basic income will initially start. Such is the vision that summarises our founding concerns at STWR, which we shall now go on to explore from a logical and intuitive viewpoint in relation to the case for a UBI.

Assuming our motivating interest is to achieve a basic income in the truly universal sense—above all, as an economic right that can prevent anyone from subsisting in poverty—then we have to begin by acknowledging the sheer magnitude of this longstanding crisis. While millions of people in rich nations are deprived of sufficient access to life's essentials, almost all those suffering from chronic undernourishment live in poorer countries, particularly across sub-Saharan Africa and Southern Asia. In many of the nations within these regions, no less than a third of the entire population suffers from hunger. And in many conflict-ridden states at the present time, record numbers of people require life-saving food and medical assistance, constituting the gravest tragedy of its kind since the inauguration of the United Nations system in 1945.

Even before this dramatic escalation of food insecurity in recent years, more than an estimated 40,000 people were dying from avoidable poverty-related causes each day, the vast majority in low-income countries.[16] Yet we know there is enough food, enough medicines, enough money and other resources to redistribute to all those in dire need—primarily from within the most developed regions of the world that oversupply and waste an inconceivable amount of food and material goods. This worsening reality of poverty amidst plenty, of luxury amidst starvation, may have existed for a long period of time; but how are we going to change the situation unless millions of citizens unite to demand that governments address it in a large-scale, systematic way?

Only through colossal demonstrations that continue for days, weeks, months and even years at a time will our elected representatives be compelled to heed the people's demand for economic sharing and global justice. And at the centre of our demands must be a call for governments to share their surplus resources with other nations, as informed by this commonsensical understanding: that there is enough for everyone, and no-one should be allowed to subsist in penury or needlessly starve. In this way, the idea of sharing surplus resources is the key for unifying world public opinion, and the word 'surplus' is very important to stress, because we are not talking about sharing those resources that we ourselves need to feed our families and live well. We are talking about the surplus resources that each nation can easily make available for a global poverty relief effort, directed towards the suffering of those who are living on the edge of subsistence within our own countries and abroad.

The urgent necessity of realising an international emergency programme has been reiterated throughout this series of studies, with frequent reference to the *Report of the Independent Commission on International Development Issues*, published in 1980 under the Chairmanship of Willy Brandt.[17] Notwithstanding the Brandt Report's outdated economic positions, its call for a massive transfer of resources from the global North to South is still of critical relevance today. Considering the vast scale of the world's humanitarian crisis, it is high time that governments commit to a multilateral effort to bring about an end to absolute poverty as 'an imperative goal' of the international community. Brandt's vision of a major summit of world leaders to plan and mobilise this agenda may have been side-lined during the heyday of market triumphalism, but its time will surely come—however altered in its finer details—as the old economic and monetary order continues to break down.[18]

In our present discussion, it is not necessary to enlarge upon the specific policies that will define a new approach to North-South development and cooperation, although it should be clear that encouraging support for this broad vision is very different from advocating for a UBI in separate countries. What we are really interested to achieve is this phenomenon of mass demonstrations taking off around the world, until the idea of ending poverty *as a people's leading priority* is in the consciousness of billions, and literally everyone is aware of this momentous cause. Imagine, if you can, the sudden arising of a new consciousness that declares: 'no more hunger, no more needless deaths!' Then further imagine the kind of popular actions and demonstrations that may ensue, in a prolonged attempt to bring about a coordinated response of the United Nations to finally end this moral outrage. But this should not be on the basis of political leaders telling the public what they are prepared to do, as with the usual communiqués and vague commitments that are released after international summits. The driving force for action must be ordinary people of goodwill who spontaneously amass, day after day and night after night for however long it takes, with the express intention of bringing governments back to reason with this most simple, humane demand.

We submit that without this historic occurrence taking place for an unrestricted length of time, there may never be hope for realising the definitive vision of a UBI worldwide. Policymakers will always find an excuse to defer its introduction, as we have long witnessed since the days of the Speenhamland system to the guaranteed income plan of Richard Nixon, and indeed the more recent Swiss referendum.[19] As long as the principle of sharing is not established in world affairs, as long as world leaders have yet to accept the need for massive transfers of resources to the global South as part of 'a programme for survival', then a genuinely universal basic income will never be achieved in any comprehensive measure.

Alas, what this depends on is a degree of awareness of the world problem that is woefully lacking among most ordinary citizens within affluent societies, and even within the affluent parts of poorer nations. Yet without a certain empathic awareness and heartfelt response to the avoidable suffering of those less fortunate than ourselves, it is nigh impossible that a UBI will eventually be sustained as an essential policy instrument for eliminating material deprivation. There may be numerous technical reasons why a full UBI scheme is arguably unfeasible in any country today, but the lack of general awareness or concern about the tragic reality of world poverty is, in the end, the most underlying causative factor from a holistic point of view.

Observe how the Americans, the French, the English, the Japanese and other Westernised nationalities are increasingly polarised within their domestic politics, which reflects the growing economic and social divisions that characterise all nations today. The problem of how to reduce those divisions and inequalities is often the subject of intensive public debates, as reflected in the nationally focused priorities of political parties during election campaigns. But what the public doesn't tend to see or think about is the inequalities between different nations and disparate world regions, and especially the pitiable life chances of the poorer half of the world. Yet only by sharing the world's resources can those international divisions be healed, which is a process that will act symbolically like a magnet to attract all manner of other social transformations, including the eventual possibility of rendering a UBI into a viable policy instrument within each nation.

Interestingly, the vision of a UBI represents the logic of economic sharing, as usually conceived of in solely national terms. However, the vision of what sharing means on an urgent global scale is only partially upheld by most UBI supporters, including the small number of organisations that have dedicated themselves to the idea of ending absolute poverty through a basic income guarantee in developing countries. Most supporters perceive a fragment of that vision of economic sharing in the context of their own country alone, without realising that a full UBI policy cannot be sustained anywhere before a global process of resource redistribution takes place among every member state of the United Nations.

The surest way to initiate that process, as we have stated, is through the active engagement of millions of people in every country who together raise their voices for an immediate end to poverty-related suffering, until the United Nations commits to an intergovernmental emergency programme and a comprehensive restructuring of the international economic system. Asking for a UBI as a solution to poverty in every country is therefore an unconscious call for sharing the world's resources, even if we fail to recognise the key for how to achieve such an epochal aim. Because that key will not be discovered until the majority of humanity embrace this cause in unison, all of which depends upon a marked expansion in our collective awareness and empathy towards others, thus to understand our poorest brethren's needs as equally important as our own.

Hence in our quest to achieve the inspirational vision of a basic income for every person within any nation, there are two possible routes to try. One is through the path of mounting resistance, where we attempt to build a countervailing political movement that forces the establishment to concede a new system of income distribution based on a UBI, with all the attendant risks of inciting tremendous state opposition and violence. Or we can take the path of least resistance, which is to build a different form of global movement altogether based on *Article 25* of the Universal Declaration of Human Rights—straightforwardly calling for adequate food, housing, healthcare and social security for all.[20]

This takes us back to the instructions contained within STWR's flagship publication, wherein an appeal is made for reviving this venerable Article through peaceful protest actions that persist around the world without cessation.[21] To summarise some relevant aspects of our reasoning, we observed how the phenomenon of global demonstrations with a unified purpose have currently reached their acme through calls to protect the environment, but never through calls to protect the fundamental rights of the struggling poor majority in less developed countries.[22] Yet it is through such a call on an unimaginable scale that we can eventually change the trajectory of world affairs, thereby opening the door for a UBI and countless other policy solutions that progressive campaigners stand behind.

Above all, the people's strategy of heralding *Article 25* is the surest way to reach the poor, the destitute, the forgotten in their multitudes—for the human rights enshrined within those few humble sentences *belong to them*, first and foremost. Thus it is possible that if the Western world protests with continual vigour for this one benevolent cause, then the poor living in marginalised regions across the southern hemisphere will also hear the call, and hopefully join in themselves.

Perhaps a similar logic might hold for the common cause of a UBI, since it is the very poor who will benefit most from a regular monetary transfer as enshrined in national legislation. But there are many reasons why protests for a UBI are unlikely to proliferate as a unified global phenomenon by themselves. To begin with, the politics of achieving the right to a basic income is generally limited to the level of the state, where social policy is crafted and implemented within each nation. The call for *Article 25*, however, is truly international in its aspiration to ensure that everyone has the basics needed to survive. Even the most conservative or business-minded individual will say they agree with *Article 25* regardless of their views on a basic income, and irrespective of what ideology they promote or political views they espouse.

Moreover, the mental ideas associated with a basic income are primarily about money and personal finance within any given society, as highlighted by the very word 'income'. Whereas the mental ideas associated with *Article 25* are concerned with moral principles and our collectively shared aspirations, recognising that (in the words of the Universal Declaration) the 'inherent dignity and the equal and inalienable rights of all members of the human family is the foundation of freedom, justice and peace in the world.' Indeed the work of implementing a UBI is really for economists and policymakers, whereas the work of implementing *Article 25* initially depends on the engaged hearts and active participation of every segment of society together. And it is through those heartfelt actions that a 'divine economist' will eventually emerge, if we can read between the lines, as embodied in the phenomenal spectacle of united global demonstrations that continue through the day and night *ad infinitum*.

Also from a technical point of view, there are many policy implications related to guaranteeing the human rights of *Article 25* that are not included within a basic income proposal. For example, how should a government generate the means for providing universal public services under democratic control—healthcare, utilities, education and so on? Most governments will clearly need to enact major economic reforms if these essential services are to be protected and augmented in every developed nation, and firmly established in every developing nation as a legal entitlement of all citizens. Due to the complexity of these issues, it is therefore pragmatic to call for an overarching political demand that encompasses all the associated policies in an uncomplicated way. Under the umbrella of *Article 25*, there must necessarily be a fusion of other political demands, all of which reflect the beauty of the principle of sharing in its remarkable diversity. A demand for meeting the basic needs of all must surely include, for example, calls for:

» the redirection of military spending and other harmful government subsidies;
» the renegotiation of unjust trade agreements;
» the clamping down on tax avoidance and evasion practices by wealthy individuals and corporations;
» the major restructuring and democratisation of global governance institutions;
» the redistribution of resources through new sources

of international taxation (on financial transactions, carbon emissions etc.);[23]
» as well as myriad other causes for economic sharing on national and local levels.[24]

In this way, the real possibility of building a global movement around the implementation of *Article 25* will have tremendous knock-on effects for related campaigns and progressive activism, which would be the blessing of all blessings for proponents of a UBI. Obviously they will gain enormous support for their endeavours, if we can anticipate an endless wave of popular demonstrations that call upon our respective governments to redistribute surplus resources to the least developed global regions. Surely if you were to reason with that newfound audience of engaged citizens about the ethical and logical case for a UBI, it is very unlikely they will disagree. And perhaps that would be the time for basic income advocates to organise their own non-stop demonstrations across the globe, premised upon the aforesaid moral justification that 'everyone has the right to live'.

From these initial observations, it may be clear that *Article 25* should form the basis of the existence of a UBI, and both should work together in tandem. It would be of tremendous help to the cause for a basic income if all its supporters were to equally embrace the cause of heralding *Article 25* in their meetings, proposals and group activism. As we have argued, when you include *Article 25*, then you include the fundamental needs of the poor in every detail—and that is how you call on the masses in all countries to join you. What is more, it is through the grand mobilising potential of *Article 25* that government policies may begin to change in the right direction, via a global call for economic sharing and cooperation to end life-threatening deprivation as a leading priority of the United Nations. It is the everyday masses in heartfelt unison that will firstly express the principle of sharing on this Earth, and it is their united demand for redistributing global resources that will eventually trigger the possibility of securing a basic income for everyone, and so much else besides.

It could be said that the principle of sharing represents the soul of a UBI, in a metaphorical sense, while *Article 25* is like its mother or parent guardian. Indeed it was the Universal Declaration of Human Rights that inspired humanity to put its house in order after the Second World War, out of which the long-held aspiration for a basic income found its natural family home. For all these reasons we have discussed and more, the basic income movement faces a long and dark road ahead of them, if they don't associate their political ideations with the established right to an adequate standard of living, and take shade under its umbrella until their opportunity comes. If you have a car, you also need petrol to drive it; there is no simpler way to encapsulate our argument. And thus it makes sense from every logical, practical and strategic angle to adopt *Article 25* if you want genuine UBI programmes to be eventually implemented worldwide.

*

It may help us to contemplate anew some of the strategic reasons for why it makes sense to herald *Article 25*, further to the rationale set forth in STWR's book of the same name. As we emphasised in that manifesto for massive civic engagement, our central aim is to indirectly bring about a metamorphosis in the profit-seeking interests that dominate every society, thus forcing major corporations to metaphorically bow and concede their hold over the governmental policymaking process. This is the issue that UBI advocates should ponder on and take very seriously in relation to their proposals, engaging with the utmost of their visionary imagination and intelligence. For we are not talking glibly about establishing a new society with free money and free love for all, as if everyone can suddenly decide to overcome their ideological differences and live without undue conflict.

Need we remind ourselves that publicly traded, limited-liability corporations of vast influence are like war machines let loose in a quest to extract profit from all human and environmental resources, with a legal obligation to prioritise profit-maximisation above moral or ethical considerations. Suppose each vision of a better world is symbolised by a house, and transnational corporations are represented by tanks unleashed in a war zone that incidentally destroy each house in turn. Thus our idealistic visions are rapidly extinguished like collateral damage in the war-like pursuit of the illusion of unlimited capital accumulation.

Such an analogy may be somewhat exaggerated, but it is the continuation of that symbolical battle which our political leaders are invariably engrossed with—as brought to life since the 1970s through their market-driven policies of privatisation, commodification, de-regulation, low corporate taxation and all other such divisive means to generate economic growth. Yet the origins of the evil of unfettered market forces goes far deeper than merely a misguided political ideology. As alluded to earlier, the human motivations that sustain the globalised economic system also represent the culmination of humanity's age-old tendencies towards greed and institutionalised self-interest, which has always been enabled by our indirect complicity and indifference throughout the generations. The question of how to release the world from thralldom to this ancient materialism is not to be taken light-heartedly—especially when considering the origins of modern capitalism through centuries of imperial rule, colonial theft and the horrific exploitation of vulnerable populations.

Are we therefore naïve to expect that humanity can ever change these seemingly engrained and selfish tendencies, simply by upholding a declaration of human rights that has never been more than a moral aspiration—as yet, non-legally binding and unenforceable as an economic obligation upon governments? Continuous global protests around the rights of *Article 25* might seem a remote likelihood, but we can at least indulge our minds with the hypothetical implications that might result from this prodigious occurrence. For what do we believe would be the principal effect on those transnational corporations that seek profit at all costs, in the midst of countless millions of people demanding that our governments render *Article 25* into a set of enforceable obligations through national and global laws? And what do we think would be the principal effect on the workings of governments themselves, bearing in mind that even our policymakers are effectively servants to those centralised corporate bureaucracies?

This is where the real war begins for achieving a full UBI, since embedded within this political cause is the need for governments to redistribute wealth to the majority populace. Hence the phrase 'progressive redistribution' immediately comes into play, for there is no way to achieve a comprehensive UBI system in the immediate term, unless governments are compelled to regulate large corporations and reclaim public resources through the kind of economic reforms we pointed to above. According to our reasoning, our greatest hope in this regard is not a nationwide public demand for the government to implement a UBI in our own country alone, but for the United Nations to guarantee *Article 25* through genuinely cooperative intergovernmental action. That is the only way to redistribute wealth and political power downwards, both within and between every nation. And that is the only way to bring about balance and harmony in global economic affairs, while preventing any UBI policy from corrupting due to the forces of commercialisation, the destructive power games of foreign policies, and the distorted priorities of governments who have no idea what it means to serve humanity.

In time, the widespread call for sharing may gradually extend its versatility into the establishment of new laws and new systems of income distribution, thus ensuring that the foremost role of governments is to defend everyone's right to a dignified livelihood and an adequate standard of living. To use another metaphor, this is not to suggest that UBI supporters are knocking at the wrong door, although we can conceive of two doors within the same building that have to be consecutively passed through. When the front door for *Article 25* is pounded by millions of people in every country, then an interior door is finally revealed, behind which lies the highest vision of a UBI with all its hopeful promises for social justice and freedom. But that second door will not require the public to symbolically knock upon it through endless demonstrations on a colossal scale—for by that time, it will open automatically by itself.

PART III

The inner dimensions of world transformation

There is another perspective that may further elucidate this relationship between a UBI and our vision of heralding *Article 25*, which is to explore the inner dimensions of how society must transform its profit-oriented values through the collective expression of love, goodwill and sharing in its multiple forms. This mode of enquiry is always of primary importance in our studies, for an emergency programme to prevent life-threatening deprivation will not only lead to transformations in the arena of political decision-making, but also profound *inner* transformations in the consciousness of humanity as one interdependent entity.

Let us put it this way: that such a momentous happening will signify the beginning of the end of most people aspiring to make millions, of wanting to become rich at the expense of others and the Earth. It will mean the rich themselves becoming involved in this great social endeavour to alleviate the needless suffering of others, galvanised by an awakening of the heart that leads to unforetold changes in terms of our intrinsic values and sense of togetherness, inclusiveness, oneness and indeed love. Even the many 'isms' that represent the opposing beliefs of our societies are likely to lessen in their extreme polarisation and gradually converge over time, in direct proportion to the arising of a newfound awareness that sharing the world's resources is the only way to save our ailing civilisation.

We can easily envision the wider repercussions for ourselves, if we accept that any such *outer* transformations clearly depend on preliminary *inner* transformations within the consciousness of humanity. For as we have postulated, these inner transformations can only be brought about by an unprecedented awakening to the reality of needless poverty-induced suffering, leading to an eventual reallocation of the world's surplus food and other critical resources to where they rightly belong.

However, it is difficult to imagine the actual experience of such a new 'sharing-oriented' or 'love-oriented' social atmosphere, when the values of our present society are effectively based on the opposite of sharing and right human relationship. When we hear people talk of 'our values' and our nation's 'way of life', it is almost meaningless from an inclusive spiritual perspective while millions of people are dying each week as a result of extreme poverty, violent conflicts and unmitigated natural disasters. What kind of values can we possibly mean in this appalling global context, if not the values that define our psychological separateness and insular behaviours? When terrorists murder innocent civilians in affluent Western cities, we often hear commentators state that religious extremists cannot divide us or destroy our values, our democracy, our so-called way of life. But are we not already divided in how we live, due to the indifference that sustains the vast inequalities in living standards worldwide?

Thus imagine the transformation in consciousness that is necessary for humanity as a whole to express awareness of our divisions on a planetary scale, until the values of right relationship begin to hold meaning in our everyday lives. We have already suggested how those new values will initially be expressed—above all, through the heartfelt awareness that no-one should be allowed to die from hunger, and a unified public demand for governments to share their surplus resources through an emergency redistribution programme. Only then can we conceive of the kind of society where a basic income guarantee is unanimously accepted and supported, but not before.

The missing element in many proposals for a UBI is therefore related to this question of our global empathic awareness and demonstrated unity, and our awareness will naturally expand in every direction when millions of people rise up under the banner of *Article 25*, guiding us towards the values of right human relationship in all its variety of forms—interpersonal, communal, institutional and otherwise. Considering that right relationship also means 'not to harm' or 'I seek to defend others and the planet from harm', it will not be long until that immense release of public awareness is directed towards the main perpetrators of planetary destruction, namely the multinational corporations with their insatiable appetite for profits and resource extraction. But what do we think will be the effect of whole societies embracing the cause of economic sharing to alleviate poverty in all its forms, with respect to exploitative business activity and profit-seeking interests?

Perhaps there will be no tangible effect as we might presume, and those vast commercialising entities will be simply left behind. For there will be such an atmosphere of goodwill and service to the world, that even many corporate executives and rich investors will leave their industries to participate in this great planetary event themselves. In time, many multinational corporations may also begin to change their business models and objectives entirely, as our awareness of the reality of global inequality is enlarged towards an awareness of the critical environmental situation, and the need for humanity to drastically reduce its unsustainable demands upon the Earth.

To be sure, the public must drive this burgeoning awareness of corporate wrongdoing and harm, which may be translated into widespread disengagement from the many industries that are profiting from human and ecological destruction. Consumer activism is a powerful defence tactic in this regard, when enormous numbers of citizens seek to challenge egregious corporate practices through boycotts, direct actions and other forms of grassroots organising. All we are really imagining is the repercussions of goodwill and awareness as it pervades every society, focused on the direction of the heart and common sense towards right thinking, right action and right human relations. From thereon, the exploitative practices of large corporations will naturally cease or be transmuted into more beneficial forms of activity, as much as the awareness of the masses begins to reflect a newly engaged and less selfishly inclined motivation.

As we have said before, the underlying problem was never capitalism or the monopolistic corporation, but only the consciousness of man that has allowed these acquisitive practices and systems to develop in harmful ways. Hence when man becomes aware of the damage that his indifference and complacency has caused, then capitalism and the corporation will change its outer modes of operation by an exactly equivalent measure. As our consciousness is transformed, so the transformations will follow in society and the global socioeconomic order. The mind shifts, the politics shift, and the world itself adapts to the shift of that shift.[25]

When we relate these observations to the cause for a UBI, we can only repeat that its stalwart supporters will soon get tired and old, unless humanity embraces the principle of sharing through continuous protest activity around the established rights of *Article 25*. The very occurrence of that event will represent the beginning stage of an expansion of our collective awareness, until the necessity of implementing a UBI becomes obvious, acceptable and eventually inevitable within each nation. As our awareness continues to expand and grow along these more altruistic lines, the very term 'basic income' may also change over time (if doesn't cease to exist), and assume a different meaning that more closely aligns with the values of right human relationship. In any case, what mental associations are conjured by the words 'basic' and 'income' within the context of a commercialised society that is adept at trivialising anything with real value, thus degrading the psychological meaning of a UBI to the level of 'pocket money' or a 'free giveaway'?

Although we cannot predict how our social perception of a UBI may evolve in the future, what should be apparent is the need to examine this subject in a far more holistic and universal light, with awareness of the inner side of life. Then our justifications for a UBI will not be limited to arguments around the coming age of automation, or the need for a less consumerist and work-obsessed society. In contrast, our starting point for understanding the path towards a UBI is to see the problem of tension between nations, and the endemic stress and depression in our societies that is holding back the expression of right human relations.

This is the clinical side of sharing the world's resources, if we can express it in such a way, since the most important outcome of sharing from an inner perspective is the reduction of international tensions, thereby enabling groups to form together on every level—planetarily, nationally, communally and interpersonally in a synergistic union. Then the true forms of cooperation can naturally proliferate, with positive results beyond all expectations in regard to the competitive relationships between governments on the world stage. It may be said that when a genuine process of economic sharing finally commences, when governments are empowered to structure an emergency programme of poverty relief through the United Nations, then the broader structures necessary for establishing right human relations will automatically begin to manifest on every level of society.

And one of the main elements for structuring the process of economic sharing involves the right distribution of income, founded upon the same principle as an international emergency programme: that we have enough resources to meet everyone's basic needs, if those resources are properly utilised and redirected to where they are most critically needed. We all know there is enough food, enough medicines, enough physical goods and technology to rapidly end all forms of material deprivation. But it is in the reality of accomplishing this great civilisational endeavour that our awareness as to what else our societies can achieve will naturally grow—just one example being the implementation of UBI schemes across the world. Then new laws will be made to sustain the new structures, which will render the puerile social arguments against a full UBI essentially meaningless and irrelevant.[26] Because then we are talking about a different kind of society altogether, where every individual is guaranteed the basic resources they require to sustain their intrinsic feeling of self-worth, and express their innermost sense of joy, freedom and creativity.

There is no need for us to go deeper into this subject here, which concerns the need for a new education as highlighted in several of our earlier writings.[27] Suffice to say that we are envisaging a more spiritual, heart-engaged and compassionate society in which the experience of stress and violence is negligible, and the Christ Principle is no longer a mere theological idea, but an experiential reality in the lives of almost everyone. When the hearts of humanity are opened, when the overwhelming levels of tension in our world are gradually reduced, then we can be sure that a basic income guarantee will assume its predestined place as an essential component of what it means to live in right relationship.

*

The preceding reflections are intended to demonstrate how a full UBI policy may never be viable in any country, unless fundamental changes take place beforehand in our collective consciousness and social values, which must eventually be reflected on a political level among the world's governments. We have now investigated the elements that are missing in most discussions around a basic income policy, and the reasons why any universal programme is liable to corrupt within the present socio-political context.

There are many connotations of danger that surround UBI proposals today, from so many different angles. As alluded to beforehand, the phrase 'basic income' itself is becoming dangerous in the commercialised societies we live, where the foreboding trends we cited earlier are continuing to worsen, not least the growth of the world population. How else are these trends to dissipate and reverse, unless we rapidly safeguard the rights of *Article 25* within all nations?[28] In light of our reasoning, we can see how the truly universal vision of a basic income appeals for so many other problems to be resolved. Indeed how dramatic are the problems that surround this simple policy proposal, unless we are talking about the affluent nations of the Western world alone.

Many UBI proponents may still remain preoccupied with the question of how to achieve their vision of a sharing society within major industrialised countries, particularly those of Western Europe and North America. But if we look at this question through the common sense of an engaged heart, it becomes apparent that a UBI scheme can never be sustained within the borders of a single nation, as long as the rest of the world remains so unequal and perpetually in conflict. Even supposing that a rich country like Switzerland were willing to provide a liveable amount of money to all its citizens (without means testing or conditions of any kind), there are obvious reasons why such a national system may pose insurmountable dangers in the longer term.

In the short term, an affluent nation may be able to prevent an influx of poor migrants through border controls and various restrictions to entitlement of a non-contributory UBI scheme, such as waiting periods and qualifications based on residency. But regardless of the pressures of selective in-migration, how long could such a system last considering the downward pressures of economic globalisation on public policymaking?[29] From the most logical analysis in this competitive and profit-driven world, there is sure to be tremendous opposition to the advancement of any nationally redistributive scheme, in whatever country it may originate.

When also examined from a purely moral viewpoint, we should ask ourselves if a UBI can ever succeed on a strictly one-nation basis, if it is not pursued in accordance with a vision of one humanity that is spiritually integrated and undivided. It is natural for campaigners to direct their proposals to a national level at first, and look towards the good of themselves and their own fellow citizens. However, a UBI must also be seen as a solution for our multilinked global problems, and be directed towards the idea of the common good of all—otherwise, our ideations are clearly not based on a universal conception of justice, solidarity, equality and human rights. For then it would be as if we regard our own country as the sum total of 'humanity', while remaining indifferent to the fate of the billions of people elsewhere who do not share our privileged national identity. And then we will be increasingly lost in a sovereign enclosure of our own making, in which our undisturbed days are numbered while the problems outside our country borders continue to multiply and worsen.

Hence it is immoral for a full UBI to be implemented by one country alone (even if they have the means to do so), in a world where poverty is rampant and many war-ravaged nations are struggling to avert soaring levels of food insecurity. It may well be possible for everyone in your own country to live comfortably with a guaranteed basic income and universal social services, but what about the others in poorer countries who do not have any such entitlements, or even a morsel to eat? If you were the prime minister of the United Kingdom and you passed legislation through Parliament to implement a high-level basic income scheme for only British citizens, would you care nothing for the people in France or Germany if they were besieged by a calamitous natural or economic disaster, leaving untold millions of your regional neighbours hungry and impoverished? Yet that is effectively the reality of how people in wealthy nations debate their domestic affairs, as if they can defend their established social protection systems without reference to the misfortune of those who live in tormented countries further abroad.

Thus we see the consequences of the lack of sharing in our world, as welfare states corrupt in industrialised nations due to all the problems associated with the paradigm of commercialisation in this peak phase of its global expression. Until around the late-1970s, countries like Great Britain may have demonstrated the inclusive potential of universal welfare states as effective sharing economies, before the ideology of unfettered market forces and private ownership began its reign in world affairs. But as we have established, sharing a *nation's* resources through redistributive policies of progressive taxation and social transfers is a very different matter to sharing the *world's* resources. And without the commencement of a process of economic sharing among every government (as never properly witnessed on this planet since the creation of the United Nations), then the existing social safety nets across the industrialised world will continue to deteriorate and corrupt.

Already we see the signs of this real and present danger, now that human life has been computerised by means-tested benefit systems that humiliate and widely fail those most in need. Those shameful controversies are preordaining a time when the public welfare systems of the twentieth century will inevitably collapse—unless, that is, our societies are dramatically reorganised on more inclusive and moral premises. With this in mind, it behoves the proponent of a UBI to campaign for their policy as a vision for every nation in unison, while remaining heedful of the reality that this cannot be accomplished until the principle of sharing is at least beginning to control the relationships between nation states. All of which returns us to our central prognosis: that the missing element for initiating this noble vision is a people's strategy for world transformation based on heralding *Article 25*.

PART IV

A definitively universal vision

Our last consideration is to examine what the highest global vision of a UBI may look like in the future, following the transformations in public awareness and international relationships that have been outlined in this discussion so far. There is certainly a value in attempting to envisage these new economic arrangements, even though it is futile to try and articulate the final policy details which will be the work of trained economists of the highest calibre (assuming this farsighted ideal is ever to come to pass). Let us not forget that the entire architecture of the global economy has to be restructured on a significantly more just and equitable basis, before the possibility of guaranteeing *Article 25* in every country is remotely conceivable.

To be sure, governments are incapable of protecting economic and social rights for all citizens without rolling back the policies of the modern period that have greatly exacerbated economic insecurity, and legitimised the privatisation of the economy. The redirection of vast military expenditures to social needs is crucial, but we must also consider the need to transform the many other policies and structures that have constrained governments of the global South since the 1980s and earlier, including the whole system of global tax havens, unpayable sovereign debts and unfair trade arrangements. By this means, it is possible to anticipate *Article 25* becoming an enforceable law of human rights within the United Nations, leading to the possibility of a UBI being seriously debated by all member states as a means for achieving such an ultimate objective. Then we may finally consider what a truly 'universal' basic income means—that is, as a global social policy tool which can help to guarantee the basic rights of every human being indefinitely.

As a point of note in this regard, many development economists are hailing the promise of cash transfer (CT) schemes as a pragmatic method of reducing poverty in low-income countries, potentially forming the basis of a new social contract between citizens and the state if scaled up sufficiently. Much evidence suggests that CT schemes can have a transformative effect on the lives of excluded citizens, whether or not they are delivered with certain conditions such as child vaccinations or school attendance. This is particularly the case for the millions of people who work in the informal sector and live in marginalised communities, typically without access to secure employment or comprehensive welfare services. For the time being, we can therefore observe how the proven success of cash transfers reflects the versatility of the principle of sharing in relation to poverty reduction strategies, even when applied in limited measures to target groups as an experiment to test for particular outcomes. In a profit-based world that is beset by artificial scarcity, access to money *per se* is invariably transformative—even for the richest individuals, which is why it is natural to expect that giving money directly to the poor will potentially transform their lives.

However, from the wholly inclusive and ideal perspective that we are pursuing in this enquiry, these targeted CT schemes should be viewed in the context of a global poverty emergency that is far from being addressed through multilateral negotiations and an intergovernmental programme of structural economic reform. The results of CT experiments point to what could be achieved through full nationwide UBI systems, although this is many steps removed from our vision of all countries agreeing to implement such schemes on a cooperative international basis. Indeed, we may be able to experiment with the poverty of excluded citizens in both high- and low-income countries, but we cannot experiment with the lives of those thousands of children and adults who are at risk of dying from hunger *in this very hour*. Periodic cash transfers will never be enough to save these countless innocent lives, unless nations commit to an emergency poverty relief programme in the immediate term, alongside the longer-term restructuring of the global economy that can address the root causes of mass impoverishment.

For now, CT schemes are best understood as an inadequate form of aid that can help soften the worst impacts of material deprivation, if only for those relatively fortunate people in developing countries who are chosen as recipients by governments or donors. But we are looking towards a time when that aid is transformed into a permanent system of basic income that benefits everyone without exception, and is eventually coordinated by the United Nations with the pledged support of all nations from both hemispheres, North and South.

At the onset of such an eventuality, it is reasonable to predict that multilateral negotiations towards this end should be held under the auspices of the United Nations. After all, if we are envisaging the need for a basic income from a truly universal perspective of human rights, then the United Nations General Assembly is the only nominally democratic and representative forum that currently exists on the intergovernmental level. And there are already many specialised agencies within the United Nations system that coordinate international efforts to promote peace, security and respect for basic human rights. So when the time comes for coordinating a UBI for all nations simultaneously, then the word 'universal', in this context, has to be associated with the foundational purposes and principles of the United Nations and its treaty obligations.

What is this venerable institution for, if not to give 'we the peoples' an equal chance for a dignified and healthy life? And in the wake of all the social and political transformations that we have summarised, the global vision of a UBI is likely to become so popularised and widely discussed that it will have to be debated within the highest political forum, for where else can it be organised on a multilateral basis? If the Security Council can be empowered to authorise military interventions and sanctions for the ostensible cause of preventing human rights abuses, then surely the more inclusive General Assembly can be utilised for the benevolent purpose of supervising the creation of UBI systems in every country. Perhaps we can even foresee the establishment of a new specialised agency that is responsible for this critical task, one that operates in conjunction with other relevant agencies as an autonomous and vital part of the United Nations family.

At this juncture, it should be stressed that we are *not* envisaging the need for a planet-wide basic income that is distributed to every individual directly via a complex centralised bureaucracy within the United Nations system. Especially not if that would involve the creation of a supranational transfer system of some variety, which may conjure an impression of a future world government.[30] On the contrary, it is imperative that every sovereign nation is encouraged to develop a UBI system in accordance with its own specific means and requirements, always respecting its unique traditions, customs and democratic practices. In that process, however, we are anticipating the need for governments to abide by agreed international laws of the United Nations that determine the general principles and standards of each domestic UBI scheme, thus guaranteeing everyone's right to an adequate standard of living (as already enshrined, of course, in *Article 25* and its related international human rights instruments).

In other words, member states can agree at the General Assembly to independently implement a UBI, one that is sufficient to eliminate material poverty and promote fundamental human freedoms. No doubt it will be long and arduous work before such a treaty is adopted, for it must also include provisions for those less developed nations that will still require international support to develop an effective UBI scheme, alongside the expansion of state-funded public services and universal welfare systems. A global solidarity fund will have to be instituted for this express purpose, which could be financed by any variety of options that are now widely discussed in progressive circles—many of which entail new and innovative methods of raising 'social dividends' from commonly-held resources.[31, 32]

Again, it is not the intention of our enquiry to examine the plausibility or acumen of existing proposals, except to observe how the global vision of a UBI is dependent on a redistribution of wealth, power and resources on an unprecedented scale, and within a dramatically short timeframe. And the extent of that redistribution has to be 'universal' in all respects, most crucially on the intergovernmental level through the cooperative pooling of surplus resources and the creation of a world public revenue. We know it can be achieved in the fullness of time, however far-fetched it may presently seem. Indeed, if nations can organise themselves to build the complex infrastructure of war, they can also cooperate to build the infrastructure of a new global economic system that is organised through the principle of sharing, and sustained by new international laws of the United Nations.

This was in fact the broad destination that Willy Brandt was aiming towards several decades ago, in stressing our interdependence and the need for nations to redirect public spending priorities from 'disarmament to development', with 'massive transfers' of resources to the world's poorest regions. We could say that the Brandt Report was indirectly calling for the structural reforms necessary to implement *Article 25*, recognising that it could never be achieved without a new spirit of global solidarity based on mutual interests and economic sharing. And in so doing, he was also indirectly presaging a time when UBI policies could be implemented worldwide, because both of these goals exist along the same trajectory, and remain connected through their same underlying purpose—to ensure 'the right to live' with dignity and freedom for everyone in the world.

When viewed in this light, however, there is an important distinction between what Brandt tried to achieve in terms of sharing the world's resources through North-South cooperation, and the most consummate vision of a UBI that can only be achieved at a subsequent stage. Evidently, the first stage concerns the relationships between nation states, and the need for a more equitable form of development to rebalance the world economic system, thus abolishing extreme poverty and laying the foundations for longer-term international security. But the second stage of implementing a UBI worldwide involves the relationships between individuals and their government, defining a new social contract that will be *reinforced* by the latterly agreed laws of the United Nations relating to *Article 25* in its general prescriptions. Put simply, it is only by sharing the world's resources that all nations—independently and yet on the basis of mutual support—can bring about the new political arrangements that are necessary for realising a sustainable vision of a UBI in all nations. For it is a vision that will never be achieved so long as vast discrepancies continue to exist in the wealth of different world regions, as per all the reasoning of our foregoing argument.

From a certain perspective, it is the wealthiest industrialised nations that are most challenged when it comes to implementing the definitive measure of a full UBI. Because even if they are dedicated to implementing such a policy within their own borders, we observed how they would be forced to exacerbate all the divisive means by which they currently maintain their ill-gotten prosperity. So unless these destructive systemic processes are gradually reversed, unless the richest nations commit to a massive programme of international resource transfers, and unless the governments of the world begin to cooperate in a genuine spirit of solidarity, then it is pointless to discuss any further the vision set out in this enquiry. There is nothing wrong with continuing to promote such a noble cause as a UBI, but we will be figuratively walking with a ball and chain until our preceding cause is firstly realised—namely, for monumental public demonstrations that continually uphold the human rights of *Article 25*.

EPILOGUE

Some final words of encouragement

Please note that the purpose of repeating the last conclusion from several angles is not because it is a fanatical belief, or a wishful future prediction, when it is actually based on a logical and intuitive analysis of what must *strategically take place*, if the highest ideal of a UBI is ever to realistically eventuate. Certainly it is admirable to fight for the cause of a basic income in the existing political climate, although it is important to understand where the crux of our challenge lies, which is ever the question of how to gather the mass majority of humanity alongside us. Advocates who embark upon this struggle have taken a pioneering and honourable path, a path that inherently says 'above all nations is humanity'. But still our problem remains a lack of sufficient public support, which would need to be at least comparable to the awareness that surrounds the environmental issue if political leaders are to take UBI proposals seriously.

Arguably the same can be said of development issues more generally, when NGOs and political activists are left fighting for the rights of the poor without sufficient backing from the public-at-large, as if these critical issues can be left to qualified professionals and our governments. Even those few politicians who attempt to represent these issues on our behalf are left fighting a losing battle, unless the masses are standing behind them with a united voice, all together for one goal. Like a cork that is pressed down into water, any political measure that promotes a redistribution of wealth will be fiercely rejected by the conservative status quo, which we must remember is not a new situation. Such has it always been, since long before you or I were born.

Only now, it seems, a different perception is arising, a newfound sense that we cannot continue with the old ways anymore. We are becoming aware that the underlying problem lies with everyone in society, in the very manner in which we think and live, which ultimately relates to the level of our consciousness as a race. Hence the problems of the world cannot be resolved by a mere handful of activists fighting against the illusions of our governments, or by NGOs who lobby politicians to change their policy prescriptions and accept alternative ideas. Let us repeat that the real changes needed must originate from within the expanded consciousness of humanity as one interdependent entity, which is a deceptively elementary conclusion with immeasurable implications for the work that lies ahead.

Further to this understanding, participants in the UBI movement should be wary of 'isms' in all their polarised forms, whether left-wing or right-wing in origin, as they are an ancient psychological problem that can be very obstructive in their nature, and thus hinder the light on our path. The question every UBI proponent should ask themselves is: am I here for humanity, or for an idea? Because if there are many different factions within the movement, all pulling in opposing directions, then it is clear that we are motivated by a cerebral *idea* that has no cohesive life within itself. And then we can be sure that our idea will remain the preoccupation of a minority of intellectuals and aficionados, while all the negative trends we cited earlier continue to worsen. Until in the end, a basic income will be regarded as a quaintly utopian idea and little else, one that is soon forgotten in the maelstrom of fragmenting societies and environmental breakdown.

But it is another matter if our reasons for participating in this movement are motivated by the welfare of humanity as a whole. In which case, the idea is not solely about 'us' or our own particular countries, and we will naturally expand that idea to the common good of all. Thus the idea will assume a life and meaning of its own, provided the pioneering groups that introduce it to the world are talking about the lives of absolutely everyone, enabling the poorest peoples and nations to join a united cause. For then we are truly conceiving of one world that is inherently equal and undivided, instead of conceptualising our basic income as a means of maintaining a relatively comfortable lifestyle for ourselves and our fellow compatriots, forcing the people in less privileged nations to sit and watch our insular campaigning activities, but nothing more.

So let not the idea of a UBI fall into the hands of university academics and intellectuals alone, who should never be supported in trying to lead any social movement that represents the humble needs of the marginalised poor. The academic may well understand the problems of humanity in intricate detail, but unfortunately they are apt to compartmentalise that understanding as if you can reduce human life into a box of ideas. And humanity is not an idea, which is why the *masses themselves* must lead this nascent global movement to redistribute our common wealth, without having to rely on the so-called leadership of a highly schooled minority. For despite the importance of intellectuals in challenging other thinkers and informing a political debate, they cannot persuasively represent the world's downtrodden masses who do not understand the sophisticated language of the intellect.

Talk to the average person in your local supermarket about a counter-hegemonic strategy to challenge the dominant theoretical framework of neoliberal capitalism, and you will observe the typically bemused response. But talk to the same person about the need to share the world's resources and uphold *Article 25* of the Universal Declaration of Human Rights, and you can be sure they will understand and nod their heads in agreement. That is why every member of the UBI movement should be very careful not to be too academic in their thinking, and not too influenced by isms and beliefs. If you try to work through the intellect alone in your attempts to change the world, it is certain that the world will change you through those same three elements—because the world is largely made of isms, beliefs and intellectual output.

We should also be on our guard against the forces of differentiation in groups, which refers to the tendency of people to increasingly lose sight of their good intentions after joining with others for a principled cause. So many groups that stand for the betterment of humanity are unfortunately susceptible to the illusions of isms, leading to the formation of different factions within the group that have nothing to do with the true meaning of goodwill or cooperation. We see this time and again within the arena of national politics, where most parties compete for power and fail to cooperate for the common good of all peoples and nations everywhere. But the same tendency can afflict civil society organisations that seek refuge in their intellectual propositions, and thus become elitist towards other organisations and the ordinary citizen whose interests, ironically, they were originally founded to represent.

In a way, it is understandable that progressive groups of every variety are often led into their separate silos of thinking and campaigning, when the general public is not standing behind them in full support of the overall cause. And the materialistic forces which currently sustain our divided world are so pervasive and overpowering, that it is easy to be pulled in every direction by this rampant dark influence that aims to distract, subdue and divide us from one another. It may even seem as if the world itself conspires to change us if we try to fight for a new society within the prevailing paradigm of commercialisation. If our only response is to promote a UBI solution by joining the internecine contest of isms and beliefs, then we can state with conviction that any such cause is doomed in advance. The freshness and magnetism of this proposal will then become crystallised through intellectuality, and thus lose its very essence or heart, allowing the reactionary objections to hold sway in popular discourse.

Hence it is imperative that proponents of a basic income engage with the attributes of their heart, and do not succumb to the glamour of intellectualism with all its inherent dangers.[33] We are all naturally accustomed to engage with our heart when seeing close friends or family, and yet the virtuous qualities of a loving heart—like tolerance, inclusivity, benevolence and empathy for the suffering of others—are often missing from our dry intellectual writings and campaigning activities. However, it is not a case of engaging with our heart in relation to a UBI policy as such; rather, we must utilise our heart's attributes towards the needs of our entire society, and then promote a UBI as a potential policy tool that can help relieve the widespread suffering of humanity. Is that not the reason why we were inspired by this idea in the first place? And is that not the reason why we continue to support this obvious method of poverty alleviation, which never originated from within a mind-created ism, but from within the simple heart awareness that says 'everyone has the right to live'?

How much simpler our activism would be if we understood that policies will never transform the world, nor intellectual ideas, for the only solution lies in the awakening of our hearts through inner awareness and self-knowledge. What is the purpose of campaigning for a UBI policy at all, if we do not know ourselves and the innate goodness that we have within? Such a simple policy prescription becomes so complex when applied to the world, because the world itself has become so complex in its outer modes of social organisation due to all the *inner* problems we have discussed—a lack of intellectual openness, a lack of unselfish concern, a lack of sharing and essential love.

Of course, an intellectual or academic will never look at a UBI in this way, many of whom view it through the lens of an ism in order to justify or reject its real-world implementation. We cannot expect to talk with such an individual and convince them to think in more inclusive and spiritual terms. And for this very reason, we should be wary of trying to change a society that has become so complicated and divided through isms. For if we try and apply our simple policy prescription to the world's interminably complex problems, again it is more likely that the world will sooner change us to become similarly complex and divisive in our thinking (presuming it doesn't reject us outright as naïvely utopian).

Clearly a UBI policy is a simple idea, an almost divinely simple idea, but its simplicity can only be sustained by the power of ordinary people when they are together, in conscious unity and wholehearted agreement. Thus we can observe how the world's problems and solutions are not the exclusive responsibility of the political class; they are really the responsibility of the public in its entirety, for it is we who continue to participate in our insular lives and social festivities while millions of people elsewhere are living in abject destitution, and widely dying from prolonged starvation.

The conception of a UBI can remain so simple in our hearts, if each and every member of this movement perceives that the real substance of a basic income policy is, in fact, love. It seems we are always dynamic in responding to ideas, but why are we not so dynamic when it comes to love? If we feel the resonance of this idea in our hearts, it means we have already responded, however unconsciously or incipiently, to the call for love. In light of all our earlier reflections on the need to apply the principle of sharing to world affairs, let us underline that these new economic arrangements must be implemented through an act of love amongst the world's citizenry, and not through the imposition of a political ism. Any such isms are poisonous within the existing social paradigm, because they can only exist alongside their opposing ideologies, like capitalism versus socialism, which predetermines the likelihood of social conflict and eventual corruption from the originating ideal.

When we talk in even hypothetical terms about the highest global vision of a UBI, we can almost instinctively feel how more cooperation is needed, how greater awareness is needed, how unprecedented unity is needed through an immense outpouring of massed goodwill. If you examine this subject with your heart and mind fused together, there is one natural conclusion you will reach: that the essence of the authentic UBI vision is to manifest love in a concretised form, and that is all. Hence the primary reason why a full UBI has yet to be implemented anywhere is due to a lack of love, for what else can it be? Everything can be simplified in this way. But the love we describe has no relation to sentimentality, or the vacuous ideals of world peace that are expressed by many New Age spiritual groups. Because in order to successfully awaken that love, serious hard work is waiting for us. And a UBI represents much more than a theoretical idea, assuming that its predestined future role is in line with all that we have envisioned—which is ultimately to spread love in this world to where it is most needed.

When examined from this inner or psychological-spiritual perspective, it can be concluded that the path to achieving a basic income is the antidote to man's indifference and complacency, because there is no way of achieving this liberating proposal without perseverance, without awareness, without inclusiveness and goodwill that is unparalleled in scope. It represents a call for unity and cooperation that has yet to be seen on this Earth, in the same way that the human body cannot function properly without unity amongst its vital parts, producing harmony among the heart, lungs and other visceral organs. Hence the UBI proponent is called upon to lead the way in that unified effort to create a more cooperative and redistributive society with a healthier heart and lungs, so to speak, considering the strength of the opposition that will inevitably seek to co-opt our principled cause for their own benefit. Just as soldiers are trained to fight in a spirit of brotherliness with their fellow troops on the battlefield, the peaceful activists for a new social settlement are called upon to advocate their policy ideas in a spirit of camaraderie and sympathy towards all other adherents, without dividing themselves in terms of isms and intellectuality.

The call is not to unite within factional alliances, which would fail to appeal to the average person of goodwill. Rather we should inwardly and repeatedly ask ourselves why we are interested in a basic income policy to begin with, if we are not ourselves demonstrating the inclusiveness and right relationship that we strive to see reflected in the outside world. The present author would like to make a tentative prediction that genuine and full UBI systems will eventually be established in every country under the aegis of the United Nations, but such a vision is currently a dubious prospect, a somewhat vague and questionable dream, so long as the majority of citizens are not interested in or convinced by its egalitarian promises. Without the ferocious support and unity among existing group members, it is logical to predict that this very fragile idea—if an idea is all that it is—will eventually collapse and be considered naively utopian for evermore.

One way to exemplify that group unity is through non-stop demonstrations and direct actions that call on our respective governments to guarantee a basic income for every citizen. But any such activities must have nothing to do with socialism or radical left-wing politics, and should instead be a reflection of our maturity, our responsibility and our common sense from the heart. If we can organise continuous conferences year on year, we can also organise continuous demonstrations that unite UBI supporters in a common cause. And thus we can embody the spirit of the popular slogan that advises in political terms: 'Don't go left, don't go right, just go forward' (although we should add: 'and always remember who you are').

Such persistent demonstrations will soon give strength to the idea, considering that billions of people throughout the world still do not know that a basic income movement exists. And those unified gatherings, however big or small in the beginning, will help to spread the word and influence other countries to follow our example. Don't forget that the primary meaning of a UBI is simply the 'right to live'—a premise, as we argued, that the poorest of the poor will most certainly agree with.

Furthermore, it is also hoped that we will be influenced by the sum of all the reasoning in this investigation, compelling us to advocate for *Article 25* and the sharing of global resources alongside our country-specific demands for a basic income guarantee. That is the way to reach the impoverished masses and empower their own voices for a better life, since we have not yet reached a time when the implementation of a basic income is feasibly international in scale.

We observed that *Article 25* is a longstanding aspiration for universal human rights that lies at the centre of the United Nation's founding ideals, which is why we must uphold it, demand it, and mobilise around it on that precise basis. If we think and strategise through the lens of *Article 25*, and if we remain sincerely guided in our hearts by the light of the principle of sharing, then there is no danger of intellectuality and isms getting in the way. The supposition is plain and simple: we must feed our starving brothers and sisters on the basis of a long-neglected global emergency, and provide everyone with adequate welfare and social services as long stipulated as a basic human right in core multilateral treaties.

Article 25 is the guiding inspiration for a worldwide UBI in these important respects, since it doesn't refer to the implementation of a theoretical idea—rather, it is pointing towards the survival of the human race, if we can construe its profounder significance at this critical time. For in order to guarantee the rights of *Article 25*, we will automatically have to address so many other structural injustices that require an unparalleled response of economic sharing, of mutual aid, of world unity and voluntary sacrifice. This is essentially the sum of our entire reasoning, which is a thesis that results from the simple logic of a unified heart and mind, however lengthy is the resulting explanation.

*

All we need say, in the end, is that our vision of global demonstrations around *Article 25* should be accepted and introduced by the proponents for a UBI, since you cannot envision a basic income for all without envisioning, at the same time, the need for a more equitable distribution of the world's wealth. None of our solutions for global justice and human rights can be realised without the actualisation of this premise, because heralding *Article 25* may be the last chance we have for establishing the principle of sharing in international affairs. As the paradigm of commercialisation proliferates by the day, it is surely logical to assume that united protests for *Article 25* must proliferate as a countermeasure. There may be no other means for influencing world leaders to sit around the table and talk, and finally agree to redistribute resources and restructure our economic systems to eradicate poverty from the face of this Earth.

We have observed how *Article 25* almost prophetically speaks of a UBI, but its voice will only be heard if we can bring about an unwavering social crusade that seeks to realise *Article 25* as the foundations of our planetary home, without which a UBI will have no foundations to speak of. It will remain like a bird without wings, or a cart without a horse that cannot move in any direction. We have tried every other strategy and nothing else will work, unless nations freely share their surplus wealth with an awareness of divinity, of the one Humanity, the one Love. That is the key we are all searching for, which has forever been embedded in the hearts of everyone.

In the last analysis, what is the most persuasive motivating factor for any member of the UBI movement, if not their soul impulse that says 'love and serve all'? Although some members may distort or degrade that higher impression through the lower impulses of their personality, still the divine conception of a basic income exists on loftier spiritual planes, awaiting the time when humanity will respond to this advanced idea with the right inspiration. There can be no greater moral or spiritual justification for promoting a UBI than the cause of feeding the hungry and relieving the suffering of the poor, for the needless perpetuation of extreme poverty is the shameful reason why millions of people are left unable to spiritually evolve. The growth of the soul through love and service is the essential reason why we incarnate on the physical plane at all, so what other motive can there be for supporting the idea of a UBI *for everyone on planet Earth?* We have often remarked that allowing millions of people to die of hunger in our midst is to deny the chance of those human souls to fulfil their inviolable spiritual purpose. And now the potential to return that God-given chance to the impoverished millions is lying in all our hands, if only we seize the opportunity.[34]

It is not a question of creating 'another possible world' as often wistfully proclaimed, for there is only one world, *this* world, and it is up to us to transform it. We cannot miraculously establish a new society overnight, but we can instantaneously establish a new awareness, a more spiritual understanding and mindset, once we are enlightened by a general knowledge of the evolving kingdom of souls. Many people believe that the fifth or spiritual kingdom of our evolution is somewhere up high on another dimension, when it actually denotes a certain state of being or awareness that every individual gradually reaches and exemplifies, from lifetime to lifetime.[35] We cannot therefore accurately describe what a better future world may look like in material terms, due to the Law of Free Will that enables man to decide for himself the mode and pace of his evolutionary advancement.

All we can predict is how that better world will originate in subjective terms, based on our compassionate awareness of the whole. For it is the extent of that heart-engaged awareness which will determine the transformed structures and relationships of our societies, upon all levels and in all their different forms. And only through such an expanded consciousness can we reach the stage of implementing a UBI on an international basis, signalling a time which may be most appropriately described as an Age of the Heart (for what does a 'New Age' mean, after all?). The phrase 'a shift in consciousness' is frequently used to describe the need for collective inner transformation, but the way our societies are presently structured means that such an occurrence may take many centuries or even millenniums, when such time is what we do not have.

Thus it appears that divine intervention is necessary to help humanity back onto its feet again, reorienting us to the simple path of intelligence, love and right relationship. Perhaps we will need a Christ-like economist to inspire the new methods and purposes of sharing our planet's bountiful wealth, if it doesn't require the reappearance of the Christ Himself to convince us of the need to dramatically relinquish our self-destructive modes of living and indifferent behaviours. But even if the Christ did declare Himself to the everyday world, it will still remain up to us to inaugurate an Age of the Heart through the eternal means of His omnipresent love. How simple and undogmatic is the true meaning of the Christ Principle, even as it brings about such an extreme polarity of reactions to the escalating crises of these climactic times. In Biblical terms it may be interpreted as the Sword of Cleavage, that which creates a confrontation of opposites between the old ways and the new—thus allowing humanity to make a final choice between the inclusive path towards freedom and justice, or the insular and competitive path that is imminently leading to the extinction of all life on Earth.

A hopeful outcome may not seem guaranteed at the present time, and so shall it remain without an outpouring of love that peacefully heralds *Article 25*, which is the certain assurance that the Sword of Cleavage will be sustained in the right spiritual direction. Then the factual reality of that Sword will be more palpable than ever before, and humanity will know more clearly the way it needs to go, despite the inevitably fierce opposition from a large reactionary segment of the population. The appropriate means for implementing a UBI worldwide will also become clearer in human consciousness, once *Article 25* is on course to being enshrined as an enforceable law of the United Nations. For as you shall recall, the symbolical mother of a UBI is represented by *Article 25*, and both are inseparably conjoined with the divine principle of sharing—although the daughter will never be born without her mother already existent in the world.[36]

The principle of sharing is the great educator for the coming Age of the Heart, although its method of universal teaching is of an unfamiliar kind, as to hear it one must learn how to think and listen through the heart. That is how we will gradually realise what sharing means in spiritual terms, for its real significance will only become apparent when we finally experience the awaited Heart Age, or what might be better described as the Age of Love. This may sound like sentimental language, but perhaps it is not too far away from all of our long-repressed childhood feelings and deepest inner yearnings. Each person has an important part to play for what lies ahead, which is nothing more than a call to use our hearts and serve others with tireless dedication and worldwide participation. The call for a UBI is precisely that in its holistic meaning, once it is interpreted and understood in a spiritual sense as a call for love, a call for service, a call for caring for one other and the Earth.

The reason we are repeatedly emphasising the spirituality of a UBI is because money *per se*, in both its material and subjective aspects, is also a form of energy that will adapt to the inner changes of individuals *en masse*, like everything else. As the material form and psychological value of money follows the gradual expansion of human consciousness, it will also therefore assume a different energetic quality, until the (socially-created) concepts of 'money', 'profit', 'income' and 'wages' will no longer exist as we know them today. When we begin to construct our societies in such a way that right human relationship holds a more tangible and articulatable meaning to everyone, then our usage and need of money will naturally begin to lessen in its prevalence.

There are some visionary groups within the activist community that anticipate a sudden transition to a money-free world, but do these idealised imaginings account for the inner side of world transformation as we've discussed? Bearing in mind that from our perspective, any such transformation must begin with the massed participation of ordinary people towards alleviating the suffering of those less fortunate than ourselves. This behoves us to be mindful that a shift in consciousness does not equate to a shift in policy ideas, or to the shifting of our government's attitudes to proposed technological solutions. The shift in consciousness we are concerned with involves the expansion and evolution of human consciousness *in the aggregate*, which can only be initiated through a collective awakening to our true spiritual nature and destiny, as immediately reflected by the unity of global demonstrations that uphold the established rights of the very poorest amongst us.

As a result of that prolonged and magnificent occurrence, the shift in consciousness we speak of will continue to expand along the correct spiritual lines, and at the most astonishingly rapid pace for innumerable individuals and families who will then know, for the first time, what it means to live with an inner experience of security, freedom, creativity and grace. Then the Ageless Wisdom teachings will become of incalculable importance for humanity as we seek to expand our consciousness in a less materialistic direction, seeking instead to unfold our awareness of the timeless spiritual verities and the reality of the existence of the soul, which may eventually be scientifically proven.[37] The meaning and usage of money will consequently evolve in such an unexpected way that no-one can make any concrete predictions at this stage. All we can ponder is the merest hints of what that brilliant future civilisation may look like, where the first signs of a more awakened and cooperative consciousness will be reflected in new macroeconomic models that are predicated on the principle of barter and exchange.[38]

The main point we are seeking to illustrate in these concluding remarks is that there is much more to the idea of a UBI than at first meets the eye, and its existence is a relatively small, transitional part of a greater whole that has yet to reveal itself to our imaginations. That transitional period may continue for a long span of time, assuming humanity finally decides to follow the lighted path that we have indicated and sparsely outlined. The path itself is infinitely long and marked by untold wonders, although we have yet to take the first step into that fateful promised land. And that step will not be taken without an explosion of love through the principle of sharing, presaging a glorious era when a worldwide UBI will definitely have its place in the evolution of humankind.

Endnotes

1. The basic income referred to in this investigation is the most ideal imaginable type, as broadly envisioned by prominent advocates and progressive campaigning organisations. The commonly accepted ideal characteristics of a basic income is that: it should be *universal* i.e. automatically paid ex ante to all legal residents of a given country or province; it should be paid in the form of a cash grant to every *individual* (including children at a possibly lower sum), and in a uniform amount i.e. with no variability according to household or family status; it should be *unconditional* i.e. provided without means testing, behavioural requirements or restrictions on how the money should be spent; and it should be transferred on a *regular* and predictable basis, such as monthly, without the threat of being withdrawn i.e. due to bankruptcy or the foreclosure of debts. These characteristics distinguish the definition of a genuine UBI from its many variants, particularly the 'minimum income guarantee' or 'negative income tax' proposals, both of which are targeted measures that may require complex means tests.

2. It is generally accepted by most proponents that a basic income should not be introduced as a means to privatise social services, or to effectively dismantle what remains of the welfare state in rich industrialised nations. STWR firmly stands behind the agreed position of the Basic Income Earth Network (BIEN), for example, in opposing 'the replacement of social services or entitlements [via the introduction of a UBI at whatever

level], if that replacement worsens the situation of relatively disadvantaged, vulnerable, or lower-income people'. While it is not the author's intention to engage with the particulars of this controversial debate, it should also be emphasised that STWR firmly supports social policies based on solidaristic and democratic principles. We therefore recognise that—within the context of the prevailing economic paradigm—the most immediate and rational response for progressive activists is often to defend collectively-funded social services and established labour rights.

3. *Article 25* of the Universal Declaration of Human Rights (General Assembly resolution 217 A): (1) Everyone has the right to a standard of living adequate for the health and well-being of himself and of his family, including food, clothing, housing and medical care and necessary social services, and the right to security in the event of unemployment, sickness, disability, widowhood, old age or other lack of livelihood in circumstances beyond his control. (2) Motherhood and childhood are entitled to special care and assistance. All children, whether born in or out of wedlock, shall enjoy the same social protection.

4. Mohammed Mesbahi, *Heralding Article 25: A People's Strategy for World Transformation*, Matador books, 2016. <www.sharing.org/article25>

5. Our exceptional focus on *Article 25* is not meant to disregard those other fundamental rights that are necessary for a dignified and fulfilling life, as embodied in the core provisions of the International Covenant on Economic, Social and Cultural Rights (ICESCR), adopted by the United Nations General Assembly in 1966. This would include those Articles associated with the right to social security, health, education, participation in cultural life, and also those labour rights that recognise the right to decent

work with adequate protections. It is noteworthy that the right to a basic income is also enshrined in the Universal Declaration of Emerging Human Rights, compiled by civil society associates on the occasion of the Universal Forum of Cultures in Barcelona 2004 and Monterrey 2007, which also recognised 'the right to an unconditional, regular, monetary income paid by the state and financed by fiscal reforms... as a right of citizenship, to each resident member of society, independently of their other sources of income, and being adequate to allow them to cover their basic needs.'

6. In part IV, we broadly consider the possibility of implementing a definitive vision of a basic income on a coordinated global scale. It should be stressed from the outset, however, that we are not envisioning a global basic income that is paid and funded by a supranational political unit of some variety, as per some of the speculative ideas promoted by a small number of scholars and grassroots organisations. While these proposals for universal worldwide coverage are unique and honourable in their focus on ending extreme poverty, it is taken for granted in our discussion that a UBI will always need to be administered, controlled and primarily funded by sovereign governments. To be clear, STWR is not advocating for a global-level system of progressive income taxation (or a more innovative proposal for raising international revenues) that acts to redistribute a basic income, via a centralised administrative agency, *directly to every citizen of the world*. In contrast, we envision an important future role for a democratically reformed United Nations—and any new agency that may be set up under its auspices to supervise the redistribution of global finances—in facilitating the process of enabling individual governments to establish full UBI schemes in their respective countries. This is the tenor of our discussion in part IV.

7. As shall become clear from part I, a full UBI is not considered politically realistic or achievable at the present time, but only viable in the context of extensive structural reforms to the global economic system. We are also considering the means for achieving a UBI as a permanent system within every country, not only as an immediate possibility (however theoretically plausible or implausible) within the most wealthy industrialised nations with established welfare states. For the purposes of our discussion, it is not therefore deemed necessary to review the many technical arguments in favour of a UBI as a proposal for individual countries under existing conditions. This would include the arguments for streamlining the provision of government benefits, for overcoming 'poverty traps' associated with targeted welfare systems, for creating a better alternative to social insurance schemes that increasingly fail to reflect the reality of precarious employment, and so on. A sizeable literature exploring these issues can easily be researched by interested readers.

8. Although this enquiry does not set out to argue the case for a UBI, it is worthwhile noting that the combination of all these factors present a compelling overall justification. As variously explained in the contemporary literature on the subject, new solutions are needed for the intractable problems associated with the relentless pursuit of GDP growth and growing unemployment. The traditional policy objective of full-time work for all who are able— based on an interdependent relationship between the state, the individual and capital that formed the post-war social contract— is no longer a meaningful response to the growing adversities of our societies in this new era of globalisation. Millions of people in the global South are now growing up without realistic prospects of employment, due in large part to global chains of production with increasing technological efficiency, rendering vast swathes

of the world population surplus to the needs of capital. Although the full scale of the future impact of technological and digital change is debateable, it is certain to bring large-scale disruption to almost every section of the labour force over time. It is also certain that developing countries are most vulnerable, where the automation of manufacturing and other industries could soon lead to a further massive displacement of low-skilled labour. Yet the elusive objective of full employment is not only unsustainable from an economic and social point of view. Even if it were possible to maintain full employment despite the continued increases in production with less labour, the planet itself cannot sustain this enduring assault on its resources. The old formula for addressing poverty and inequality—to produce more, work more and grow the economy more so that people can consume more resources—has already pushed humanity to the very brink of (if not beyond) the ecological limits of growth. Hence in our search for a new macroeconomic model that resolves these contradictions, a UBI may represent a significant part of the answer as to how steady-state economies and simpler lifestyles can be achieved. Indeed, to the extent that it disassociates income from productive contribution, a UBI points the way to an alternative vision of a sustainable society—one that even John Maynard Keynes hesitantly dreamt of in the 1930s, where we can share work more widely and enjoy an age of leisure, instead of blindly pursuing the path of ever-increasing wealth. Thereafter the nature and purpose of work can be reconceptualised, enabling people to prioritise those things that matter most: rebuilding communities and nourishing relationships, caring for one another and the Earth, exploring the spiritual meaning of our lives through voluntary simplicity and the art of living. In time, therefore, technological progress can eventually be a means to free humanity from its thralldom to materiality, whereby the basic needs of society are produced with maximum material efficiency and minimal human labour, while full UBI schemes help to ensure that the fruits of machine-produced wealth are equitably shared. This represents an essential vision of a more emancipated, participatory and egalitarian world that appears to be dearly embraced by many UBI proponents, including the present author. However, the ponderable question that underlies our discussion concerns the means by which humanity may safely reach this hopeful vision in light of the foreboding trends that are summarised in part I.

9. What amount of money may be necessary to ensure an 'adequate standard of living' is a complex question, and it may vary greatly between countries and remain subject to democratic debate and adjustment. In general terms, however, the monetary value of a UBI can be understood as 'basic' in the sense that it will provide a fundamental level of economic security to every citizen, or a 'social floor' that is sufficient to cover all essential needs (in combination with the public funding of universal social services and other welfare programmes—see note 2). We are thus envisioning the possibility of a 'full', 'liveable' or 'high-level' UBI in the most consummate and universal sense within each nation, while remaining mindful of the fact that partial or introductory-level schemes may be the most pragmatic route to achieving this end goal. It is beyond the scope of our discussion to take a position on whether a full UBI should replace existing contributory social insurance schemes altogether, as well as other non-contributory social protection measures for the poorest in society. At this stage, common sense would attest that neither the specific amount of a full UBI should be given too much importance, nor the specific structure of UBI schemes that may also vary greatly between countries in their final forms. It should certainly not be taken for granted that a basic income must automatically replace all existing transfers and other forms of state benefit.

10. Johannes Ludovicus Vives (1492-1540) is in fact attributed as the first to develop an argument and a detailed plan for a minimum subsistence scheme, as early as 1526. In a memo to the mayor of Bruges, titled *De Subventione Pauperum* ('On Assistance to the Poor'), he writes of nature and its resources: 'All these things God created, He put them in our large home, the world, without surrounding them with walls and gates, so that they would be common to all His children.' More than two centuries later, Thomas Paine (1737-1809) famously developed the essential idea underlying the basic income concept, namely the notion that the aged and indigent deserved public assistance not as charity but as a right, which should take the form of a basic endowment that is distributed to all. 'Poverty... is a thing created by that which is called civilized life. It exists not in the natural state,' writes Paine in his pamphlet *Agrarian Justice*, where he argues the case for: 'a National Fund, out of which there shall be paid to every person, when arrived at the age of twenty one years, the sum of fifteen pounds sterling, as a compensation in part, for the loss of his or her natural inheritance, by the introduction of the system of landed property.' In Paine's immortalised words: 'It is a position not to be controverted that the Earth, in its natural uncultivated state was, and ever would have continued to be, the common property of the human race.'

11. In contrast to the usual descriptions of a 'basic income', the term 'dividend' is more preferable for many reasons, as long advocated by earlier academic theorists such as G.D.H. Cole and James E. Meade, as well as many contemporary writers such as Guy Standing, Peter Barnes, Charles Eisenstein, James Robertson and several other Georgist thinkers. By framing the policy in this way (in Cole's words, 'as a dividend payable of right to all citizens as their share in the common heritage of mankind'), it is more likely to gain widespread public support on the grounds

of social justice, recognising that a basic income should indeed be a universal right based upon the collective wealth of society. This rationale is notably different to the old labour principles of social solidarity, based on direct contributions and pooled risk-sharing mechanisms, which underpinned social insurance schemes in the nineteenth and twentieth centuries. Not only is the idea of 'dividends for all' more likely to overcome prejudicial opposition to the idea of 'free money for nothing', but it also naturally aligns with the most progressive options for funding such schemes—taxes on land value, a levy on royalties and licenses from intellectual property, sovereign wealth funds based on the sale of non-renewable natural resources (or other forms of common assets), and so on. However, the term 'universal basic income' is used throughout our discussion due to its familiarity and growing popularity during this new phase of its evolution. It is clearly the most identifiable term in common usage, while the word 'universal' also aligns with the moral aspirations enshrined in the Universal Declaration of Human Rights.

12. The issue of affordability is somewhat controversial, and there is no straightforward answer as to whether a basic income for every citizen is fiscally compatible with an expansive welfare state under existing conditions. Most studies that attempt to model the introduction of a UBI are looked at in a budget-neutral context, and are often based on the assumption that it will replace most other (if not all) cash benefits for working age households. On this basis, a UBI is unlikely to prove an effective means of reducing poverty and inequality, given the fact that a limited welfare budget would be spread equally across the whole population (or to all individuals below normal retirement age), leaving the poorest households with less financial support than existing guaranteed minimum-income benefits. But there are a number of larger considerations, particularly the question of how

progressive the UBI system will be, and whether it will be funded by taxing higher-income earners proportionately more. Other administrative and cost savings also need to be accounted for, including the removal of means-testing and behaviour conditions, and the full or partial consolidation of other programmes and tax credits that the new transfers would make redundant. Most of all, the question of government spending priorities needs to be considered, and the possibility of switching expenditures from regressive subsidies paid to other areas, particularly the military, agribusiness and fossil fuel industries. Although difficult to quantify in economic models, it is certain that subsidy shifting could free up enough government revenue to justify a UBI that keeps all households above the relative income poverty line, even on the assumption of fiscal neutrality. However, the full or liveable UBI that we are envisioning is no doubt unfeasible without a much wider transformation of the economy, and the implementation of alternative means to fund truly unconditional basic income schemes. For more on this issue, see note 31.

13. Mohammed Mesbahi, 'Commercialisation: the antithesis of sharing', Share The World's Resources, April 2014. <www.sharing.org/commercialisation>

14. This line of enquiry forms the basis of many of our previous studies on the principle of sharing. For example, see: 'A discourse on isms and the principle of sharing', July 2014; 'The intersection of politics and spirituality in addressing the climate crisis', June 2016; 'Christmas, the system and I', December 2013. All can be read online at: <www.sharing.org/studies>

15. The world population growth projection cited here is by no means inevitable, as also argued in our book *Heralding Article 25*, op. cit., pp. 46-51. Estimates from the United Nations forecast a population increase from the current 7.5 billion people

to 9.7 billion by 2050, with a mid-range projection exceeding 11.2 billion by 2100 (almost all in poor countries, according to the 2015 revision of figures released by the United Nations Department of Economic and Social Affairs). Yet through a just redistribution of the world's resources and the universal implementation of the human rights enshrined in *Article 25*, it is foreseeable that the conditions will be created for the world population to drop significantly over time (through natural and voluntary means). This is borne out by the evidence of population levels decreasing and stabilising when families enjoy an adequate standard of living, as historically demonstrated during the transitions from underdeveloped to developed countries.

16. In 2012, STWR calculated that around 15 million people die needlessly each year from poverty-related causes. Calculations were based on figures from the World Health Organization (Disease and injury regional estimates, Cause-specific mortality: regional estimates for 2008). Only communicable, maternal, perinatal, and nutritional diseases were considered for this analysis, referred to as 'Group I' causes by the WHO. Ninety-six percent of all deaths from these causes occur in low- and middle-income countries and are considered largely preventable. See Share The World's Resources, *Financing the Global Sharing Economy*, October 2012. <www.sharing.org/financing>

17. Willy Brandt, *North-South: A Program for Survival*, MIT Press, 1980. See also: Willy Brandt, *Common Crisis, North - South: Co-Operation for World Recovery*, The Brandt Commission 1983. London: Pan 1983.

18. Following The Brandt Commission's proposals, leaders of eight industrialised and 14 developing nations gathered in Cancun, Mexico, in October 1981 for a summit aimed at breaking the deadlock in years of protracted negotiations on the problems

related to world poverty. The hope was that representative heads of state would meet in an informal setting for two days, thereby creating the momentum and goodwill that would permit global negotiations to advance. In the end, however, no firm proposals materialised and the demands of Southern countries for a global reallocation of resources remained unmet. US President Ronald Reagan notably rejected the summit's aims to bridge the wealth gap between the few industrialised nations and the majority of poorer countries. While not all of the Brandt Commission's recommendations remain appropriate today (particularly its emphasis on increased trade liberalisation and 'global Keynesian' fiscal stimulus policies in an era when we are fast approaching environmental limits), there is still much that policymakers and civil society campaigners can draw from its 'program of priorities' and its vision for a more equitable world. Above all, this includes the proposed five-year Emergency Programme that would necessitate massive resource transfers to less developed countries and far-reaching agrarian reforms. The Commission also called for a new global monetary system, a new approach to development finance, a coordinated process of disarmament, and a global transition away from dependence on non-renewable energy sources. To date, governments have yet to realise Brandt's vision of a multilateral process for 'discussing the entire range of North-South issues among all the nations, with the support and collaboration of the relevant international agencies' (*Common Crisis*, 1983).

19. The Speenhamland system was a temporary amendment to the Poor Laws at the end of the 18th century that applied to a region in Berkshire, England. Introduced by prime minister William Pitt to address the rural poverty and hardship arising from soaring food prices, it could be viewed as one of the world's earliest basic income pilot schemes, entitling the poor within the

borders of a municipality to a cash benefit that supplemented what they earned up to a subsistence level, at a rate fixed to the price of wheat and paid out per family member. At the time, the scheme was the subject of a significant and controversial scholarly debate, with considerable opposition from prominent thinkers—Thomas Malthus, David Ricardo, Edmund Burke, Alexis de Tocqueville, G.W.F. Hegel and others—who generally favoured private charity giving over the principle of giving the poor a right to public assistance without a compulsion to work. A Royal Commission Report published in 1834 condemned the Speenhamland scheme as 'a universal system of pauperism', and recommended an end to all poor relief outside the workhouse. Thus began the era of the New Poor Law in England, characterised by insufferable conditions in workhouses that were intended to deter any but the truly destitute from applying for relief, as famously depicted in the novel *Oliver Twist* by Charles Dickens. Yet somewhat remarkably, the infamy of Speenhamland's experiment resurfaced around 150 years later, when in 1969 president Nixon attempted to push an ambitious public assistance program through Congress that would have guaranteed a minimum income to all households. According to later accounts, it was the criticism of the Speenhamland System in Karl Polyani's influential book, *The Great Transformation* (1944), that deterred Nixon from his plans, leading to the inclusion of employment or job-training requirements in return for state benefits—notoriously described by Nixon during a televised broadcast as 'workfare' instead of 'welfare'. Somewhat ironically, the Royal Commission Report that Polyani had taken on oath was re-examined by historians in the 1960s and 1970s, and was found to be based on unsubstantiated evidence and faulty methodology. More recent scholarship shows that the Speenhamland System may actually have been a relative success in reducing poverty and providing some level of economic security across the region, despite the fact that its allowances were not distributed in a reliable manner or on a genuinely universal basis. But still the myth of the workshy and feckless poor has continued to endure until this day, deterring widespread acceptance of the idea of unconditional monetary transfers to all, as again witnessed during the world's first national referendum on a UBI in Switzerland, June 2016. Although the referendum attracted unprecedented international debate, it was the assumption that a UBI would have to give every Swiss citizen a liveable amount of 2,500 francs a month (around US $30,000 a year)—an incorrect fact widely popularised by the media—which largely dissuaded popular support, with 78% of voters rejecting the proposal. In this light, it is again worth noting that almost all serious advocates see a 'full' basic income (i.e. an amount sufficient to cover basic needs) as an unrealistic goal to achieve in a single leap, and instead opt for some variant of a 'partial' basic income as the most feasible initial step (i.e. a universal scheme that starts from a very low base, or a targeted scheme for selected groups that is gradually extended to everyone).

20. See notes 3, 4 and 5 above.

21. *Heralding Article 25*, op cit.

22. Ibid, see Part III: The environment question
<www.sharing.org/article25#part iii>

23. See note 31.

24. As written in *Heralding Article 25*, op cit., p. 74: 'So let's take the path of least resistance and jointly herald *Article 25*, knowing that this is the surest route for impelling our governments to redistribute resources and restructure the global economy. Such a demand can be expressed in our own creative ways, safe in the knowledge that it holds within itself all the answers we are trying

to find. Then we may realise that many existing demands of global activists are already embodied within the Universal Declaration of Human Rights, including in wealthy countries where the call for sharing is now being expressed in an incipient form. Observe in this regard the diverse movements for accessible social housing, for the public control of utilities and transportation, for the free provision of healthcare and higher education, or for a more equal and redistributive society through fair taxation. There is no doubt that the principle of sharing must be institutionalised within each nation along these preliminary lines, and it is natural that engaged citizens are engrossed with the furtherance of these issues in their own societies. But we also have to be aware that our problems are essentially the same as those of other nations, for it is that awareness which will bring us together and make us into an implacable (although *peaceful*) international force.

25. cf. *Heralding Article 25*, op cit., p. 87.

26. For example, the moralistic objection that a basic income would be giving the poor 'money for nothing', based on the assumption that recipients of state benefits should be required to demonstrate responsibility and reciprocity, usually through an obligation to work or other job-seeking conditions. Similarly, there is the widespread and prejudicial notion that giving cash to the needy will lead to private spending on 'bads', such as alcohol and cigarettes, at the expense of spending on basic essential needs (another moralistic presumption that is widely disproven by the research findings from cash transfer schemes). A more complex and somewhat technical objection, yet one still based on a prejudicial notion of human beings as inherently indolent, is that an unconditional and obligation-free basic income will lead to disincentives to work. Basic income advocates have devoted a lot of energy to refuting this concern about a reduced labour supply, employing both logical arguments and empirical analysis. Many

argue that a UBI will actually remove the disincentives to work that already exist with targeted welfare programmes, in which claimants are threatened with the withdrawal of means-tested benefits if they take on low-paid or part-time jobs, leading to so-called 'poverty traps'. Indeed, advocates envision that a UBI will instigate a truly free market for labour, where citizens have greater freedom to choose their vocation, where greater creativity is unleashed, and where new incentives are created for employers to automate mundane jobs, or make them more attractive through greater pay. The empirical evidence that a basic income reduces the supply of labour, typically drawn from experiments in North America during the 1960s and 1970s, is also based on narrow assumptions about the nature of work. While the (often minor) changes in the level of paid work is carefully studied, the effect on unpaid work—caring for children and relatives, undertaking further education to better oneself, community volunteering and so on—is generally not considered in these econometric analyses. Yet it is the growth of these other forms of work that is of significance when considering the emancipatory effects of a basic income guarantee. For then we are talking about a world in which human labour is increasingly 'uncommodified', to adopt the language of economists, meaning that we do not need financial incentives to work, and paid work is no longer exclusively sacralised. Our passions may become our vocations, our conception of work can be redirected towards activities with real value and meaning, our innate tendency to serve others can be cultivated and rewarded—all of which has little to do with a vision of human beings as selfish, lazy and undeserving.

27. See in particular: '*The commons of humanity*', April 2017; '*The true sharing economy: Inaugurating an Age of the Heart*', November 2016; *Heralding Article 25*, Part IV, op cit. All these publications are available online at <www.sharing.org/studies>

28. See note 15 above with regards to world population trends.

29. These are the two major reasons why a full UBI scheme is both politically unrealistic and economically unsustainable under the existing conditions of globalisation. Firstly, the implementation of a genuine scheme is endangered by selective in-migration, which is likely to pressure a country with open borders to make any basic income guarantee less generous and more conditional, thus countering the threat of nativism and the problem of becoming a so-called 'welfare magnet'. Secondly, this downward pressure is reinforced by the 'race to the bottom' in labour, environmental and tax regulations, which is a distinguishing feature of economic globalisation in its present form. To give one example, corporate income tax rates have declined dramatically over the past three decades in countries of both the global North and South, in addition to the hundreds of billions being lost each year due to various forms of tax avoidance and evasion. The revenue base of the public sector has invariably suffered as a consequence, and the situation shows no sign of improvement due to the deepening trends of corporate lobbying, pro-business fiscal policies and a lack of effective global tax cooperation. While this enables an unprecedented accumulation of individual wealth and growing market concentration within the corporate sector, it is proving increasingly unfeasible for governments to maintain a strong safety net and universal social policies, let alone the prospect of introducing a generous basic income for all citizens.

30. This point is also emphasised in note 6.

31. The financing of a global fund may take many forms, including overseas aid that flows from wealthier nations to meet the enormous needs of the global South in providing education, healthcare, energy, infrastructure etc., alongside the need to

establish national basic income programmes. The requirement for a large-scale transfer of resources from the global North to South is likely to remain necessary for some years, and there are numerable options for how to raise international finances in the short term (ideally transferred through automatic mechanisms, as notably proposed by the Brandt Report—see note 17). In particular, the possibility of implementing global forms of taxation have long been discussed among economists. Examples include levies on: international trade, the arms trade and military spending, air travel and freight transport, various types of financial transactions, or the use of the 'global commons' (ocean fishing, sea-bed mining, offshore oil and gas drilling, the use of space orbits etc.) In more recent years, a number of scholars have also developed innovative proposals for creating a permanent source of public revenue (aside from taxes on labour and profits), in accordance with the social dividends approach, i.e. based on the recognition that all citizens have a right to income from 'natural property', such as land and other resources that are either inherited or co-created by society. The simple idea at the heart of most proposals is to charge user fees on shared resources, which can then be distributed to all citizens as a commons-based right. An administrative agency set up for this purpose could operate independently of both the private and public sectors. Often conceived of as a 'commons trust', it could potentially manage the usage of a range of shared resources—from land and fossil fuels, to the electromagnetic spectrum and intellectual property. While the principle of raising public revenue from the value of commonly-owned resources is usually conceived of in national terms, it can even be applied to the international level. In theory, a portion of the revenues raised could be distributed per capita to national governments as a basic income for all, reflecting the right of every person to a fair share of the global commons. Perhaps the most feasible application of this principle on a global scale is to the emissions of carbon dioxide, given that the atmosphere is clearly a globally-shared resource, and there is an urgent need to address the threat of global warming through cooperative intergovernmental action on a fair and equitable basis. Along these lines, there are some visionary proposals for global carbon emissions to be capped at a certain threshold, with emissions rights sold to the highest commercial bidders for a given period, before the revenues are distributed equally to every citizen (via a climate commons trust that operates as a multilateral institution). However the mechanism of distribution is conceived, it is eminently possible that a global system of user fees on carbon emissions could help to generate a world public revenue, while encouraging a shift from fossil fuels to renewable energy. If user fees on the global commons are distributed internationally as social dividends, it would also provide substantial financial transfers for developing countries as an automatic right, acting as an effectual compensation for rich countries disproportionate use of world resources. There are, of course, many other ideas for how to generate more equitable and stable sources of global public finance, such as the creation of a genuine international currency, issued by a world monetary authority, that provides an alternative to the hegemony of the US dollar and other reserve currencies. All such reasonable ideas indicate that the time is approaching for a global system of income redistribution (or indeed *pre*-distribution through user fees on the exploitation of the Earth's finite resources) to help provide a guaranteed standard of living for all.

32. Further to the above note, what is most important to emphasise from STWR's position on this subject is the question of how to actually achieve a progressive policy solution on this planetary scale, and without it becoming corrupted in the longer term. Thus we must invariably return to the inner dimensions of world

transformation, which always brings us back to the need for a new education on the science of the heart and the spiritual evolution of human consciousness (a far more important subject that underlies this series of studies on the principle of sharing). Prior to our discussion in the epilogue, let us repeat here that an idea alone is never enough to transform the world, especially if that idea is centred on the need for the world's wealth to be redistributed from rich to poor. For the rich as well as the poor need to be educated on the purpose and meaning of our lives (as informed by the Ageless Wisdom teachings), before the consciousness of humanity can begin to expand in a different direction, where the very ideas of 'distributive justice' or 'wealth redistribution' are eventually replaced in our consciousness by an understanding of our inherent equality or 'oneness' in spiritual evolution. No global policy idea for the common good of all can be implemented without this change in human awareness, for as long as the personality is involved, as long as violence is involved, as long as competitive greed and materialistic desire are involved in human affairs, the vicious circle will inexorably continue. A vicious circle that is not defined by the ecological limits to economic growth, but by the human limits to 'commercialisation growth' that is the real and underlying threat to our planet's future existence. From the author's standpoint, this line of enquiry is more illuminating than any debate on policy solutions, because it is the question of inner transformation that points the way to the true solution to our civilisational problems—a solution based on the principle of sharing as a divine antecedent to the consciousness changes that we sorely anticipate. And when that principle is released through worldwide demonstrations for *Article 25*, as we have attempted to forecast and encourage, then many of the policy proposals for a better world will seemingly undergo a U-turn, and assume a different sense of urgency and immediate practicability in accordance with the exigencies of the time. For what do we think is the first thing that policymakers will discover, in the wake of that momentous occurrence? The answer is the resubmission of the essential proposals contained within the Brandt Report, although this time in an enlarged design that simultaneously accounts for the world's environmental crises—for both the poverty and environmental crises now require an emergency mobilisation of all the world's peoples and governments. We merely repeat a summary of these observations to give some added context to the above note on suggested methods of world public financing, for without these aforementioned changes to the consciousness of mankind, there cannot be the level of trust or consensus that is needed to restructure the global economic system, nor the necessary modicum of world goodwill. Let us not forget that ongoing appeals from the United Nations to avert famines, conflicts and natural disasters are often critically underfunded, in a world that is wealthier and more technologically advanced than ever before. Where, then, shall the money be redirected if governments miraculously agree to devise an innovative system of global taxation or user fees on commonly-held resources? In a world of increasing militarism, commercialisation and corporate monopolisation, we can be certain that any revenues raised will not be diverted towards funding essential public services or UBI schemes in every nation. So it is not the innovative idea that will provide a lasting solution to world problems, when the underlying problem is defined by a generalised lack of public interest and social participation. That is why great world teachers like the Christ have long said, in effect: each and every one of you has a part to play in the creation of a new peace and freedom. And that is why every idea for improving the world situation is extremely worthwhile, even though it is not the idea itself that is of most value, but rather the effort that is being made to awaken the goodwill, the awareness, and the love in other people.

33. Namely, an intolerant criticism of others, the creation of divisive factions and a consequent loss of vision.

34. For example, see: *Heralding Article 25*, op cit; 'A discourse on isms', November 2014. <www.sharing.org/isms>

35. Each kingdom in nature grows from the one below it, and a fifth kingdom higher than the human—known as the spiritual kingdom or 'kingdom of souls'—has always been with us (as taught by Christ Himself), and is now gradually precipitating on the physical plane. As explained in the writings of Alice A. Bailey, that kingdom is 'composed of all those who down the ages, have sought spiritual goals, liberated themselves from the limitations of the physical body, emotional controls and the obstructive mind. Its citizens are those who today (unknown to the majority) live in physical bodies, work for the welfare of humanity, use love instead of emotion as their general technique, and compose that great body of 'illumined Minds' which guides the destiny of the world.' (*The Externalization of the Hierarchy*, Lucis Press Ltd, 1957).

36. With regards to this overall argument, readers of our other writings may note a discernible relationship between the evolving intellectual conceptions of the commons, the sharing economy and a universal basic income. All are connected in two parallel ways; firstly, through their analysis of the originating problem of commercialisation (based on the profit motive). And secondly, through their unconscious awareness of the fact that the solution for humanity's problems lies (both materially and spiritually) in the principle of sharing. However, the deeper spiritual significance of the relationship between these three political concepts may not become consciously apparent to the intellectual thinker, before the coming together of humanity through continual demonstrations around the cause of guaranteeing *Article 25*, as

variously described in this series of studies. See in particular: *The Commons of Humanity*, op cit; *The True Sharing Economy*, op cit. <www.sharing.org/studies>

37. The Ageless Wisdom refers to an ancient body of teachings regarding the energetic structure of the universe, the evolution of consciousness in man and nature, and the spiritual reality of our lives with an emphasis on 'right human relations'. It has been described as the golden thread that connects the esoteric or hidden teachings that underlie the major religious traditions, while providing the inspiration for the arts and sciences throughout the ages. Although thousands of years old, the teachings are referred to as 'ageless' rather than 'ancient' due to their progressively revelatory nature that is given active expression in people's own lives and experiences. Over the past century, a modern adaptation of these teachings has spread widely in the West following their release to the general public by H.P. Blavatsky, founder of the Theosophical Society, and later through the work of Alice A. Bailey, Helena Roerich and Benjamin Creme, among others.

38. For another perspective on this subject, see: '*The true sharing economy*', op cit.

ABOUT THE AUTHOR

Mohammed Sofiane Mesbahi is the founder of Share The World's Resources (STWR), a civil society organisation based in London, UK, with consultative status at the Economic and Social Council of the United Nations. STWR is a not-for-profit organisation registered in England, no. 4854864

Editing and research assistance: Adam W. Parsons.

For more information about STWR, please visit www.sharing.org

'How much simpler our activism would be if we understood that policies will never transform the world, nor intellectual ideas, for the only solution lies in the awakening of our hearts through inner awareness and self-knowledge.'